W

LETTERS

From a man with too much time on his hands

Mark Hebblewhite

summersdale

THE WIND-UP LETTERS

Summersdale Publishers Ltd
46 West Street
Chichester
West Sussex
PO19 1RP
UK

www.summersdale.com

Printed and bound in Great Britain

ISBN: 1-84024-534-4
ISBN 13: 978-1-84024-534-9

Mark Hebblewhite

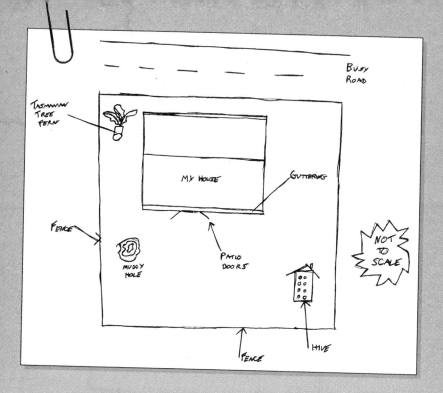

BUSY ROAD

TASMANIAN TREE FERN

MY HOUSE

GUTTERING

FENCE

MUDDY HOLE

PATIO DOORS

NOT TO SCALE

HIVE

FENCE

4

Mark Hebblewhite
Belmont Hill
Douglas
Isle of Man

British Beekeepers Association
Dr Ian Davis
Landi-Kotal
Brinsea Road
Congresbury
Bristol
BS49 5JJ

25th June 2005

Dear Dr Ian

I am writing to ask your advice on a number of issues that I hope will eradicate the problems I have been experiencing since I took up my hobby almost a month ago. My interest in beekeeping as a hobby was sparked by an article in a Sunday magazine which pictured a beekeeper in the full traditional 'uniform'.

I have constructed a hive approximately 4 feet high (48 inches) in accordance with the magazine picture. Please would you look at the scale diagrams I have included with my letter – they are in the 'plan' format and should be viewed how an eagle might see my back garden.

The hive is sited in a sunny area of my garden which I am assuming is an ideal position. Could you advise me where I can purchase bees together with an approximate costing. In time I would like to produce enough honey for my partner to enjoy on a slice of toast each weekday (including bank holidays) but not at weekends as she has sandwiches. I would be grateful for any assistance you can offer me in getting my hobby off the ground.

Yours faithfully

Mark Hebblewhite.

Mark Hebblewhite

THE BRITISH BEEKEEPERS ASSOCIATION

Registered Address: National Beekeeping Centre, Royal Agricultural Showground, Stoneleigh, Warwickshire. UK   CV8 2LG   ☎ 02476 696679

Registered Charity No. 212025

Dr Ivor Davis
Chairman
Landi-Kotal
Brinsea Road
Congresbury
Bristol
BS49 5JJ
Tel: 01934 832825
Email :
ivor.davis@btinternet.com

Mr M Hebblewhite

Douglas
Isle of man

12ᵗʰ July 2005

Starting Beekeeping

Dear Mark

Thank you for your letter dated 25ᵗʰ June. I am sorry to have taken so long in replying to you. I am very pleased that you are considering taking up beekeeping and impressed that you have already constructed a hive. Unfortunately the internal dimensions of a beehive must be very accurate to ensure that the frames holding brood and honey can be removed easily.

Before you try to find some bees I suggest you go along to some beginners classes to find out more about beekeeping. I suggest you contact the Secretary of the Isle of Man beekeeping Association who will have all the details you need about keeping bees. His details are:

Daniel Kneale
▓▓▓▓▓▓
Kirk Michael
▓▓▓▓▓▓   Tel: ▓▓▓▓▓▓▓▓▓

Good luck with your beekeeping. The honey is good but keeping bees is much better.

Yours sincerely

Ivor Davis

Mark Hebblewhite
Belmont Hill
Douglas
Isle of Man

The British Beekeepers Association
Dr Ivor Davis
Chairman
Landi-Kotal
Brinsea Rd
Congresbury
Bristol
BS49 5JJ

15th July 2005

Dear Dr Ivor

Thank you for your response to my letter dated 25th June 2005. I am very sorry to have called you Dr Ian in my previous letter. This is because I have recently purchased a new computer and all the keys look very similar at this stage. Many thanks for passing on the contact details for Mr Kneale – however, I regret to inform you that since my original letter my partner has gone off honey and now prefers peanut butter. This being the case I have smashed up my painstakingly constructed hive and have taken up darts instead on Tuesdays.

I am also conducting various experiments with vinegar's healing properties. Once again thank you for your time and should you ever decide you would like to take up darts or would like to see the results of my vinegar experiments please feel free to contact me.

Yours faithfully

Mark Hebblewhite.

Mark Hebblewhite

Mark Hebblewhite
Belmont Hill
Douglas
Isle of Man

British Alliance of Healing Associations
Mr Ken Baker
7 Ashcombe Drive
Edenbridge
Kent
TN8 6JY

25th June 2005

Dear Mr Baker

I am writing to you in the hope that you can assist me with a bone of contention that has arisen between myself and a member of your organisation. After repeated attempts to resolve the dispute, which I will outline shortly, I was given the address of your organisation by directory enquiries staff as a possible means to resolving this conflict.

To give you the brief details of my complaint I took a pair of brogues into your members' store and requested that they be fitted with a pair of long soles, new heals, and a replacement upper for the left shoe.

I paid in advance and returned 3 hours later to collect my shoes only to find that they had been given to another customer by mistake. The member of staff was rude and unhelpful and refuses to compensate me for the loss of my property nor refund the repair fee as I was not able to produce a receipt.

I would be grateful if you could advise me how I can pursue this matter.

Yours sincerely

Mark Hebblewhite.

Mark Hebblewhite

Dear Mark,

As you will notice we are a healing organisation and subsequently have no knowledge of shoes/repairs etc. I suggest you again refer to D.E staff for the right group.

May I wish you satisfaction in your endeavours.

Regards / God Bless you.

Ken Baker.

I am writing to you in the hope that you can assist me in a matter of contention that has arisen between myself and a member of your organisation. After repeated attempts to resolve the dispute, which I will outline shortly, I was given the address of your organisation by directory enquiries staff as a possible means to resolving this conflict.

To give you the brief details of my complaint I took a pair of brogues into your members' store and requested that they be fitted with a pair of long soles, new heals, and a replacement upper for the left shoe.

I paid in advance and returned 3 hours later to collect my shoes only to find that they had been given to another customer by mistake. The member of staff was rude and unhelpful and refuses to compensate me for the loss of my property nor refund the repair fee as I was not able to produce a receipt.

I would be grateful if you could advise me how I can pursue this matter.

Yours sincerely

Mark Hebblewhite.

Mark Hebblewhite

Mark Hebblewhite
Belmont Hill
Douglas
Isle of Man

British Alliance of Healing Associations
Mr Ken Baker
7 Ashcombe Drive
Edenbridge
Kent
TN8 6JY

7th July 2005

Dear Ken

Thank you for your response to my letter dated 25th June.

I cannot apologise enough for the confusion I have caused ref my enquiry regarding shoe repairs. This, as you are probably well aware, was a simple grammatical error on my behalf, perhaps as a result of my dyslexia. I am now aware that you are a healing group in the spiritual sense and this being the case are you able to assist me with overcoming my lingual difficulties?

Yours faithfully

Mark Hebblewhite.

Mark Hebblewhite

Mark Hebblewhite
Belmont Hill
Douglas
Isle of Man

Promail Ltd Mailroom Technology
Units 12/13
Network 43
Buckingham Court
Buckingham Road
Brackley
Northamptonshire
NN13 7EU

27th June 2005

Dear Sir or Madam

I am writing to inform you of a concept which I feel is about to revolutionise the mail sorting industry.

I have recently invented a mail sorting device which is currently in the submissions stage at the patent office. This being the case I would like to present you with the opportunity to look at my design and trial it with your customers on a 6 month 'free of charge' basis once the first model is completed in approximately 2 weeks.

I first came up with the concept of 'the letterinerator' whilst employed in the local government offices sorting mail. I realised that the time spent sorting mail could be better utilised performing other office duties, such as filing, if the entire sorting process was combined in one piece of equipment that was able to perform all mail sorting functions with absolute minimal input from office staff.

Please find enclosed my diagram of my Postsortertron type machine which when viewed along with the following instructions will convince you of the need to market this product to your customers.

1) Mail goes from letter box onto chute leading to machine's access point

2) Electric eye reads address on letter (or parcel)

3) Rotator fires mail into named out-trays which can then be collected by the recipient or delivered whilst staff are passing the addressee's desk on their way to the toilet, for example.

I feel that my device could lead to the extinction of office juniors.

I look forward to your response. Please do not hesitate to contact me if you require further details of my invention.

Yours sincerely

Mark Hebblewhite.

Mark Hebblewhite

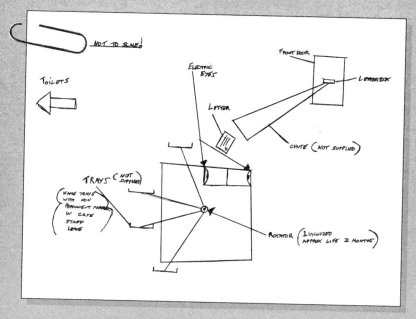

ProMail
MAILROOM TECHNOLOGY

Mr Mark Hebblewhite

Douglas
Isle of Man

21 July 2005

Dear Mark

Many thanks for sending your information regarding the machinery you have been developing. I must say I am intrigued to your design and in fact it may also have another application which is sought in the mailing industry.

I would appreciate the opportunity to discuss your project further and have the possibility to view and to see if a relationship between yourself and Promail is worthwhile for all concerned.

I will be on holiday week commencing 25th July so please feel free to call the following week.

Kind regards

Stephen White
Managing Director

Promail Ltd. • Units 12 & 13 • Network 43 • Buckingham Court • Buckingham Road • Brackley • Northamptonshire • NN13 7EU
Telephone: +44 (0)1280 709590 • Facsimile: +44 (0)1280 706200 • Email: sales@promail.co.uk • Website: www.promail.co.uk
Registered in England: 3320047 • VAT Registration: 705536837

Mark Hebblewhite
Belmont Hill
Douglas
Isle of Man

Stephen White
Promail Ltd
Units 12/13
Network 43
Buckingham Court
Buckingham Road
Brackley
Northamptonshire
NN13 7EU

26th July 2005

Dear Stephen

Many thanks for your reply dated 21st July to my letter dated 21st June. I am pleased to inform you that my Postsortertron prototype machine is now ready for your perusal. I am also pleased to announce that your very letter was handled by the machine in question which is in my hallway and was delivered to myself by my wife who was passing through the hall on her way to the kitchen in order to fetch a Pot Noodle.

I am very excited at the prospect of a mutually beneficial relationship between myself and Promail and I am most heartened that you are intrigued by my design. Further to your letter, please advise on the other application sought in the mailing industry that you feel my device is capable of performing. On your return from holiday, which I hope you have very much enjoyed, I would be most pleased to visit your premises and perform a demonstration. Please advise of a date and time agreeable to yourself. In the meantime I have composed a short verse which I do hope you are able to adopt as your company anthem for use after staff meetings. It should be sung as a group effort to the tune of ABC's eighties hit 'Shoot that poison arrow', a tape of which I would be happy to supply if you are unsure of the tune.

Promail has the answers
To industry needs
Mailing, sorting, folding
A multitude of deeds

Efficient inexpensive ways
To banish fear, nay terror
Of damaged postal items caused
By operator error

A firm and able leader
Unrelenting in his might
Come together ye employees
Show your faith in Stephen White

I look forward to your response.

Yours faithfully

Mark Hebblewhite.

Mark Hebblewhite

Mark Hebblewhite
Belmont Hill
Douglas
Isle of Man

Correspondence
Conservative Campaign Headquarters
25 Victoria Street
London
SW1H 0DL

27th June 2005

Dear Mr Howard

I am writing to invite you to an event which I am arranging on 17th July at 7pm in order to raise money for a local animal charity. Whilst the venue is as yet undecided I am trying to gain a commitment to attend from members of the business and political worlds in order to raise the profile of the event.

In keeping with the cause the event is to have an optional 'birds of prey' fancy dress theme. I would be extremely grateful if yourself or a representative could attend the event and show your support for these 'winged warriors' which are steadily decreasing in numbers despite their protected status. In return I can guarantee an interesting evening with the added bonus being that in accordance with your status you will be seated closer to the buffet.

I look forward to your response.

Mark Hebblewhite.

Mark Hebblewhite

THE OFFICE OF THE LEADER OF THE OPPOSITION

HOUSE OF COMMONS
LONDON SW1A 0AA

Mark Hebblewhite, Esq.

Douglas
Isle of Man,   July 1st, 2005

Dear Mr Hebblewhite

Thank you for your letter of June 27th inviting Michael Howard to attend your event on July 17th.

Sadly he is unable to join you as he is already commitment that evening, but I do hope the evening is a success.

Yours sincerely

Jonathan Hellewell

Jonathan Hellewell
Private Secretary

Jonathan Hellewell
Correspondence
Conservative Campaign
Headquarters
25 Victoria Street
London
SW1H 0DL

8th July 2005

Dear Jonathan

Thank you for your prompt reply with regard to my 'Birds of Prey' evening.

Further to my previous letter dated 27th June, I appreciate Mr Howard is a busy man and I regret that he will be unable to attend. However, the date of the event is flexible if Mr Howard or a representative is free on another evening of your choosing. Thank you in anticipation.

Yours faithfully

Mark Hebblewhite.

Mark Hebblewhite

Mark Hebblewhite
Belmont Hill
Douglas
Isle of Man

Pot Noodle Ltd
Freepost NATE
Milton Keynes
MK9 1BR

3rd July 2005

Dear Sir

I would very much like my children to enjoy pot meals on occasion without the current fuss that their weekly Pot Noodle 'fix' generates. As a family of committed vegetarians, due to the lack of vegetarian Pot Noodles available we currently have to rinse the flavourings from the noodles under a hot tap and leave them to dry overnight on a Tuesday before adding our own flavourings and resealing the pot so the children may enjoy them at school.

Please could you let me know if there are any plans to introduce a vegetarian range. As a family we would suggest apple, onion and gruyere, Lisa's favourite is butternut and polenta sausage, whilst in an ideal world I would opt for buckwheat, fresh figs and walnut flavour.

I can appreciate that due to market demand it would perhaps not be possible to produce a vegetarian range on a regular basis. This being the case would it be possible to produce a one-off batch for us to enjoy? It really would be a touching gesture from a large company and I would be willing to bear whatever expenses you would incur in this one-off production.

I look forward to your response.

Yours sincerely

Mark Hebblewhite.

Mark Hebblewhite

Mark Hebblewhite
Belmont Hill
Douglas
Isle of Man

Duracell Consumer Services
Freepost OF1503
Aylesbury Road
Thame
Oxon
OX9 3LJ

7th July 2005

Dear Sir or Madam

Allow me to introduce myself. I possess the largest private collection of domestic and household batteries in the United Kingdom and I am keen to share my collection and unique knowledge with all those who share my fascination.

I started my collection in 1978 at the age of six and over the years I have amassed over 17000 batteries ranging from limited edition Canadian PP9 types to French AAAs, including misprints in which the voltage listed on the side is a massive 150 volts!

During September of this year I will be embarking on a tour (limited to the UK at first) with the rarities of my collection and giving an informed talk, which I anticipate to last no more than half an hour in order that I am able to visit as many interested parties as possible.

I would be extremely grateful if you could circulate these details to all of your employees and get back to me with your 1st, 2nd and 3rd choices of date together with the venue, time and number of interested parties.

Yours sincerely

Mark Hebblewhite.

Mark Hebblewhite

**Gillette
Group UK
Limited**

Gillette Consumer Relations
Calder House
599 Calder Road
Edinburgh
EH11 4GA

Gillette - Grooming	0800 174543
Gillette - Toiletries	0800 374685
Duracell	0800 716434
Oral-B	0800 7311792
Braun	0800 7837010
Gillette - Ireland	1800 509448

22 August 2005

Mr Mark Hebblewhite

Douglas
ISLE OF MAN

UK

Dear Mr Hebblewhite,

Thank you for contacting us regarding your tour.

Thank you for extending your invitation to us for such interesting project!
We sincerely regret to inform you that we are unable to attend your exhibition during
September.
We wish you all success in your tour and would also like to send you a voucher to show our
appreciation for your kind invitation.

If we can be of assistance in the future, please contact us on our FREE PHONE at 0800 716
434 or if you are calling from Ireland, on 1800 509 448. Our hours are Monday through
Friday 9:00 AM - 5:00 PM.

Yours Sincerely

Rodolfo Pereira
Customer Service Advisor

010223771A
Enclosure:1 £10 Voucher

    DURACELL

A Subsidiary of The Gillette Company Registered office: Gillette Corner, Great West Road, Isleworth, Middlesex TW7 5NP
Registered in England Under Registration No. 265048

Mark Hebblewhite
Belmont Hill
Douglas
Isle of Man

Equity
Membership Services
Guild House
Upper St Martin's Lane
London
WC2H 9EG

10th July 2005

Dear Sir or Madam

I am writing to enquire about the possibility of joining your organisation. I am employed full time on a trainee basis by Blackpool Circus School as a human cannonball as well as participating in less specific forms of general entertainment. I would like to join your organisation but I am not sure of the experience and/or references you may require. Also I am not sure whether or not I am eligible to join as my position is currently as a trainee and in order to secure a 2-year contract I still need to pass my probationary period in order to prove I am the right calibre for the job. I would be very grateful if you could send me more details of your organisation together with any membership benefits package that is available. Should you require any further information you can contact me on 0555 123123 or at the above address. Should you require any references please contact:

Recruitment and Training
Blackpool Circus School
228 Inver Road
Blackpool
Lancashire
FY2 0LW

Yours sincerely

Mark Hebblewhite.

Mark Hebblewhite

Equity

75 years of
performing
for you

1930
2005

Mark Hebblewhite

DOUGLAS

18/07/05

Dear Mark

Equity Full Membership Application (N00241558)

Further to your enquiry, I am delighted to enclose a copy of our full membership application form. I have also enclosed a pre-paid envelope for your use.

There is a joining fee of £25 and the current minimum subscription is £90 for a year, although you can pay in quarterly instalments. Subscriptions can also now be paid by direct debit for as little as £7.50 a month – a direct debit mandate is on the rear of the form. If you chose to pay by direct debit, your application may take slightly longer to process.

Your full time trainee contract does entitle you to join Equity. Please enter details of your employment in Section 1 and enclose a copy of your contract.

If you have any questions about your application please do not hesitate to get in touch using the contact details below.

I look forward to hearing from you soon.

Best wishes,

Matt Hood
Membership Relations & Recruitment Co-ordinator

mhood@equity.org.uk
020 7670 0266

Guild House • Upper St Martin's Lane
London • WC2H 9EG
T 020 7379 6000 • F 020 7379 7001 • Mcom 020 7379 5557
E info@equity.org.uk • Web equity.org.uk

Equity
Independent Trade Union
Incorporating the Variety Artistes' Federation
Affiliated to the TUC, STUC and FIA

President Harry Landis
Vice Presidents Graham Hamilton, Jean Rogers
Honorary Treasurer Bryn Evans
General Secretary Ian McGarrv

Mark Hebblewhite
Belmont Hill
Douglas
Isle of Man

Matt Hood
Membership Relations and Recruitment
Equity
Guild House
Upper St Martin's Lane
London
WC2H 9EG

19ᵗʰ July 2005

Dear Matt

Ref N00241558

Thank you very much for your prompt response to my letter requesting details of how to join your organisation. Unfortunately in the interim period between my initial letter and your response, I have been fired by Blackpool Circus School due to poor attendance and general troublemaking. I fear that I am now in a position where I may not be able to join Equity as I am not in any form of paid employment aside from at the local sandwich shop. In my new role at Mrs B's I produce filled rolls in full view of customers with more panache than usual, in that I am prone to exhibiting impromptu juggling of sandwich fillings. I am also able to slice a baguette in two from 6 metres away (provided the shop is half empty, so as to minimise the risk of casualties). Is there any possibility that this could be considered a performance type role as I am very keen to join? I would be most grateful if you could use your influence to permit me to join, ideally on some sort of reduced subscription basis where I could provide your lunch once a week instead of a cash payment directly to Equity. I look forward to your reply and hopefully a list of your favourite sandwich fillings.

Yours faithfully

Mark Hebblewhite.

Mark Hebblewhite

Mark Hebblewhite
Belmont Hill
Douglas
Isle of Man

Mr Trevor G Lord
Parish Clerk
Foxhall Parish Council
15 Berry Close
Purdis Farm
Ipswich
IP3 8SP

10th July 2005

Dear Trevor

My wife and I will shortly be moving to the parish and would very much like to contribute to community activities and organisations. I am fully qualified in the instruction of Ju-Jitsu, and I have taken an active role in leading more traditional activities in my local pensioners group, including brass rubbing and crown green bowls. I would be very grateful if you could provide me with the details of any local organisations who may wish to benefit from my skills. Also, if you are aware of any demand for the above activities in the village that are currently not available, perhaps we could establish some new associations.

I look forward to your response and hope to hear from you soon.

Yours faithfully

Mark Hebblewhite.

Mark Hebblewhite

Brightwell Foxhall and Purdis Farm Group Parish Council

Please reply to

Trevor Lord
15 Berry Close
Purdis Farm
Ipswich
Suffolk
IP3 8SP
Tel 01473 270431

Dear Mr Hebblewhite,

Thankyou for your letter of 10 July.

I have made enquiries of Councillors and others around the area as I have no details of any of the activities that you mention within the 3 parishes and have myself moved here only 2 years ago.

Being a semi-rural area and on the fringe of the County town, it would appear that most activities such as martial arts are located in Ipswich.

Crown green bowls is mostly centered around the midlands and north of the country. Here in East Anglia we play flat green bowls, indoors and out but there are no clubs within the 3 parishes and again I would sugest that the demand for bowls is currently catered for elsewhere. (There is a major Indoor/outdoor club in Ipswich just 3 miles away).

Having said that, I cannot confirm whether there is a demand in this area for the activities that you mention, as I don't believe the residents have been asked. Perhaps that could be explored in the future.

Yours sincerely,

Trevor Lord.

Mark Hebblewhite
Belmont Hill
Douglas
Isle of Man

Brightwell Foxhall and Purdis Farm Group Parish Council
Trevor Lord
15 Berry Close
Purdis Farm
Ipswich
Suffolk
IP3 8SP

29th July 2005

Dear Trevor

Many thanks for your reply to my letter dated 10th July. From your reply I gather that the Ipswich area is already inundated with people who enjoy martial arts, flat green bowls and brass rubbing. Could I suggest that we could keep people in the parish from travelling to outlying areas to enjoy these activities by holding a sort of Triathlon (comprising of the above activities) on the village green (open to residents only) in order to bring the community together. I would be most grateful if you could discuss this idea with your fellow committee members and get back to me with your thoughts on my idea. On a final note, if the parish is not able to utilise my skills I may have to consider withdrawing my commitment to moving to the area and look for property elsewhere, unless of course there is a demand for a Smurf collectors club (I have over 237 at this time).

I look forward to your response.

Yours faithfully

Mark Hebblewhite.

Mark Hebblewhite

Mark Hebblewhite
Belmont Hill
Douglas
Isle of Man

Corrugated Sector
Confederation of Paper Industries
1 Rivenhall Road
Swindon
Wiltshire
SN5 7BD

10th July 2005

Dear Sir or Madam

Ref Mr Jones

I am writing to ask for your assistance on a personal issue which I feel you may be able to help with.

I am trying to locate a gentleman who came to view my house when it was on the market approximately 2 months ago. The gentleman in question, a Mr Jones, advised the estate agent that he was a member of the Corrugated Packing Association which I have been led to believe now comes under the jurisdiction of your organisation. During the viewing a number of personal effects were stolen from the property including my cat. I would be extremely grateful if you could provide me with any assistance with this matter in the form of the present whereabouts of Mr Jones.

Yours sincerely

Mark Hebblewhite.

Mark Hebblewhite

cpi confederation of paper industries

Corrugated Sector

Mr Mark Hebblewhite

Douglas
Isle of Man

27 July 2005

Dear Mr Hebblewhite

Ref. Mr Jones

I have received your letter of 10 July. You are quite correct in your understanding that the Corrugated Packaging Association (CPA) is now part of the Confederation of Paper Industries (Corrugated Sector).

I am sorry to hear about your circumstances but I regret that we are unable to assist. We represent a large number of member companies with thousands of employees and we are not able to trace every one of them. We would also have to consider the possibility that your visitor was not being truthful about his link to CPA, or indeed his name.

I can only suggest that you discuss this with your Estate Agent – I assume that Mr Jones had an appointment, organised by the Agent. They may possibly have more information.

Yours sincerely,

Andrew Barnetson
Corrugated Sector Manager

paper performs, *naturally*

INVESTOR IN PEOPLE

Confederation of Paper Industries Ltd 1 Rivenhall Road, Swindon, Wiltshire SN5 7BD
Tel: +44 (0)1793 889600, Fax: +44 (0)1793 878700, Email: cpi@paper.org.uk, Web: www. paper.org.uk
A company limited by guarantee. Registration Number 3886916. Registered in England and Wales
Registered Office, 1 Rivenhall Road, Swindon, Wiltshire SN5 7BD

Mark Hebblewhite
Belmont Hill
Douglas
Isle of Man

Andrew Barnetson
Corrugated Sector Manager
Confederation of Paper Industries Ltd
1 Rivenhall Road
Swindon
Wiltshire
SN5 7BD

29th July 2005

Ref Mr Jones

Dear Andrew

I am writing to thank you for your reply to my letter dated 10th July. I am delighted to inform you that since my original letter my cat has turned up. It appears that she went under the bath and up through the cavity wall into the loft where she was storing the other personal effects that I believed were stolen by Mr Jones, perhaps in preparation for the comfort and security of her forthcoming litter. I cannot apologise enough for my suggestion that a member of the Corrugated Packing Association would perform such an heinous act and I am so sorry for the false aspersions and shame I have inadvertently cast over your organisation. By way of apology I would like to invite you to become godfather for two of the kittens and also to suggest names. You can rest assured that when they are older I will tell them all about their 'Swindon connection'. Once again many thanks for your help and I hope to hear from you soon.

Yours faithfully

Mark Hebblewhite.

Mark Hebblewhite

Mark Hebblewhite
Belmont Hill
Douglas
Isle of Man

Royal Mail
Customer Services
Freepost
RM1 1AA

10th July 2005

Dear Sir or Madam

I would be grateful if you could advise me on the following postal dilemma I am facing.

On 29th October it is my mother's birthday and due to commitments at work I am unable to attend her party as I am a very busy man. I would be grateful if you could advise me how much it will be to send 2 kippers and ½ oz of Golden Virginia to Yarborough Crescent in Lincoln. I would very much like these items to arrive 20 minutes apart so as to heighten the excitement for my mother. If possible I would also like the postman to sneak round the back way past the dustbin in order to give an element of surprise. Please could you advise me of the approximate costings in order that I can make her day.

Yours sincerely

Mark Hebblewhite.

Mark Hebblewhite

Royal Mail

Glasgow Contact Centre
PO Box 740
GLASGOW
G2 1XX
Website: www.royalmail.com
Telephone: 08457 740 740
Textphone for the deaf and hard of
hearing: 08456 000 606

Mr Mark Hebblewhite

Douglas
ISLE OF MAN

Dear Mr Hebblewhite

Thank you for your recent enquiry regarding sending items for your mothers birthday in October.

It may be helpful if I explain that kippers may be sent through the post and that packages of fish should be smoked or chilled. They should be sealed in vacuum packs before posting. In all cases they must be enclosed in adequate polystyrene containment to prevent contamination. We would also need to know the weight of the package to confirm a price. I have enclosed a leaflet for your information.

With reference to your delivery request, unfortunately we are unable to deliver items with a staggered delivery time.

Thank you for contacting me about this matter and I hope you will find my reply both helpful and informative. If I can be of any more help however, please contact me again.

Yours sincerely

Janet Turner

Janet Turner
Customer Service Advisor

Enclosures: Pricing Made Easy

Mark Hebblewhite
Belmont Hill
Douglas
Isle of Man

Janet Turner
Royal Mail
Glasgow Contact Centre
PO Box 740
Glasgow
G2 1XX

6th August 2005

Ref 1-1494214631

Dear Janet

Thank you for your letter dated 2nd August regarding my mother's birthday and for the informative postal charges leaflet. I have made the pricing information into a graph so I am able to see approximate costings at a glance. I am a little disappointed that the postman will not be able to deliver articles with a staggered delivery time but I will get round this by posting the kippers and the tobacco 20 minutes apart so they are processed at your sorting offices 20 minutes apart and thus arrive 20 minutes apart. I would like to thank you for your kindness in responding by inviting you to my mother's party. There will be a buffet served from 8pm onwards and she is hoping for at least 20 guests. I am afraid I will not be there as I have work commitments but I will tell her I have invited you. Please could you forward me a list of your favourite sandwiches in order that you are not disappointed, as otherwise she will only make egg ones.

I look forward to your response.

Yours faithfully

Mark Hebblewhite.

Mark Hebblewhite

Mark Hebblewhite
Belmont Hill
Douglas
Isle of Man

Ann Summers Group
Gold Group House
Godstone Road
Whyteleafe
Surrey
CR3 0GG

11th July 2005

Dear Sir or Madam

I am writing to congratulate your organisation on giving my wife one of the most enjoyable nights of her life. Last Saturday she attended one of your parties with a group of friends and on her return it really was a pleasure to see that she had enjoyed herself for the first time in a while. Many thanks to the organiser whoever she may be. On a final note I would like to suggest an idea for your catalogue which both my wife and I feel would be a winner. We both very much enjoy a game called 'lucky burglar' on occasion in which I disguise myself as a housebreaker and force entry into our property at a prearranged time to ravish my wife. I have found it is very difficult to acquire the relevant clothing for the role, ie stripy top and mask, and we feel it could make a profitable contribution to your company. I would be pleased to hear your thoughts on my ideas.

Yours sincerely

Mark Hebblewhite.

Mark Hebblewhite

Ann Summers

VG/AEP/2107

21st July 2005

Mark Hebblewhite

Douglas
Isle of Man

Dear Mark,

With reference to your letter dated 11th July regarding your new line idea.

We are very pleased that your wife enjoyed her Ann Summers party experience, our Party Organisers are trained to a high standard but it is the fun personalities of the party guests that often make an Ann Summers party an enjoyable evening. Thank you very much for your idea for our product range, we are always considering new ideas that are both fun and sexy and our dress up range is one of our most popular pages in our catalogue.

We truly value our customer feedback and feel that this helps us shape our product range into a selection that will bring our customers the most pleasure.

Kind regards,

Vanessa Gold
Buying Director

Gold Group House
Godstone Road
Whyteleafe Surrey CR3 0GG
Tel +44(0)1883 629629
Fax +44(0)1883 629220
annsummers.com
www.knickerbox.co.uk

Ann Summers Ltd Registered Office: Gold Group House, Godstone Road Whyteleafe, Surrey CR3 0GG. Registered No 1034349

Knickerbox X Ltd Registered Office: Gold Group House, Godstone Road Whyteleafe, Surrey CR3 0GG. Registered No 2677878

Mark Hebblewhite
Belmont Hill
Douglas
Isle of Man

Vanessa Gold
Buying Director
Ann Summers Group
Gold Group House
Godstone Road
Whyteleafe
Surrey
CR3 0GG

Ref VG/AEP/2107

26th July 2005

Dear Vanessa

Thank you for your letter dated 21st July. I am a little disappointed that you didn't sound too keen on my 'lucky burglar' costume idea. Nevertheless I have plenty of other great ideas for your company's product range which I am more than happy to share with you. As a special treat on my wife's birthday I have been known to pelt my wife with sausage rolls whilst dressed as Enver Hodxa, the former dictator of Albania whose reactionary Stalinist regime brought misery to thousands and thousands of ordinary people except my wife who thought he had nice hair. (A flowing white robe is a must for authenticity's sake.)

I look forward to your comments on my idea which I am sure would be a winner, particularly amongst proactive supporters of former tyrants.

Yours faithfully

Mark Hebblewhite.

Mark Hebblewhite

Mark Hebblewhite
Belmont Hill
Douglas
Isle of Man

British Soft Drinks Association
20-22 Stukeley St
London
WC2B 5LR

17th July 2005

Dear Sir or Madam

I am writing to you because I have recently purchased a bottle of Volvic mineral water and I have a query which I feel you may be able to address for me.

Last Saturday my partner and I decided to go for a walk (past the garage and towards the large hill that we can see out of the window). After completing approximately one third of the journey, I decided to stop for a refreshing drink. At this stage I must point out that my partner wanted to wait a while longer before quenching her thirst as she said it would be more satisfying if we waited. To cut to the chase, it was a hot day and between us we managed to consume the entire 500ml immediately.

Anyhow, I have always had an eye for detail and upon reading the label on the bottle I noticed a helpline number. Even though it was a very hot day (on a par with Barcelona, according to the Daily Mirror), I knew it would be inappropriate to ring the helpline to request a 'one-off drop' in order for us to complete our journey. In addition to this my partner's mobile telephone was not working correctly due to the proximity of the hill.

To get to the crux of my query, upon rummaging in my partner's handbag I discovered a small carton of Ribena (small in that I have quite large hands due to my childhood swimming escapades). After a heated discussion with my partner, we decided to take a small sip each and pour the remainder of the Ribena into the empty Volvic bottle in order to preserve some refreshment for the remainder of our walk.

Whilst I appreciate your company cannot condone such an act would you as a representative of the Soft Drinks Association put my mind at rest by telling me that my actions on the day were acceptable in light of the fact that it was such a hot day/nice walk and it would have been a shame to ruin it.

I look forward to your response.

Mark Hebblewhite.

Mark Hebblewhite

Ref :

The British Soft Drinks
Association Ltd

20 - 22 Stukeley Street
London WC2B 5LR

TELEPHONE
020 7430 0356
FACSIMILE
020 7831 6014

Mr Mark Hebblewhite

Douglas
Isle of Man

22 July 2005

Dear Mr Hebblewhite

Thank you for your letter of 17 July 2005.

BSDA always recommends that each of us should stay properly hydrated as part of maintaining good health, and we are happy to support the Expert Group on Hydration in its work on the subject.

I enclose a copy of a factsheet published by the Expert Group on Hydration which outlines the reasons for staying hydrated and explains how easy it is to do so. Small steps can make a big difference to health and well-being.

Thank you again for writing.

Yours sincerely

Richard Laming
Public Affairs Manager

E-MAIL
bsda@britishsoftdrinks.com
WEB SITE
www.britishsoftdrinks.com

Director General : Jill Ardagh
Registered in England No. 500979
Registered Office as above
VAT No. 222213228

The importance of hydration

Many people may be dehydrated without even realising it.

An average adult should aim to drink at least 6-8 glasses (2 litres) of fluid a day to maintain good hydration. 62% of people are not drinking enough[1].

Water is also found in many foods, such as fruit and vegetables, and these are needed in addition to the 6-8 glasses (2 litres) of fluid a day.

A 65kg/10 stone person has 40 litres of water in his/her body.

We are each made up of 70 per cent water.

Human blood = 95% water

Human brain = 75% water

Human bones = 22% water

Human skin = 70% water

Being effectively hydrated helps:
- the skin
- the brain
- the heart
- the digestive system
- the kidneys and urinary tract

Email: info@experthydration.com
Tel: 020 7808 9809
www.experthydration.com

[1]TNS - 10
nationw...

---

expert group on
hydration

Each day, the average adult loses:
- 1.25 litres via urine
- 0.5 litres via sweat
- 0.5 litres via breath
- 100ml via faeces

In high ambient temperatures or if exercising a person could lose much more fluid. This fluid needs to be constantly replaced if we are to remain healthy.

Symptoms of dehydration:
- Thirst
- Dry mouth
- Decreased urinary output
- Reduced tear production
- Headache
- Cognitive impairment
- Lethargy
- Constipation

Knowing there is a choice of drinks to stay hydrated can help people meet their 6-8 glasses (2 litres) a day.

Pee Chart

1
2
3
4
5
6
7
8

Your target is to make sure that your urine is the same colour as numbers 1, 2 or 3. Colours 4 and 5 suggest dehydration and 6, 7 and 8 severe dehydration.

Weight vs necessary hydration level

All kinds of drinks, including bottled water, squash, carbonated drinks, fruit juices, juice drinks, tea, coffee and milk, can help provide the fluid needed to stay properly hydrated.

Email: info@experthydration.com
Tel: 020 7808 9809
www.experthydration.com

Mark Hebblewhite
Belmont Hill
Douglas
Isle of Man

Richard Laming
Public Affairs Manager
British Soft Drinks Association
20-22 Stukeley Street
London
WC2B 5LR

26th July 2005

Dear Richard

Many thanks for your most prompt response to my letter dated 17th July and also for the Expert Group on Hydration information card which you kindly enclosed. I am both pleased and proud to inform you that it (the card) has pride of place on my fridge door (Firenzi model number PX21), low enough for the cats to read without straining their necks but high enough to deter unwelcome pawing which may damage the laminate finish. To cut to the chase, I really must know if your organisation could sanction the specific use of an empty Volvic mineral water bottle for the containment of Ribena in an emergency situation as although I have read the informative literature you have sent, I am still unclear as to whether my actions on 10th July were negligent.

Yours faithfully

Mark Hebblewhite.

Mark Hebblewhite

Mark Hebblewhite
Belmont Hill
Douglas
Isle of Man

British Lubrication Federation
Berkhamsted House
121 High Street
Berkhamsted
Herts
HP4 2DJ

17th July 2005

Dear Sir or Madam

I am currently in the process of installing a cat-flap/pet entry system for my cat Little Pea. I say currently because during the process I have managed to get my arm stuck in the hole as I have quite large arms. I would be grateful if you could advise me of a suitable lubricant in order that I can free myself and carry on with my ordinary day to day activities. I look forward to your swift response, not least because mail is piling up around me and although it is keeping me warm it is most uncomfortable.

Yours sincerely

Mark Hebblewhite.

Mark Hebblewhite

United Kingdom Lubricants Association Ltd

Berkhamsted House,
121 High Street,
Berkhamsted, Herts.,
United Kingdom
HP4 2DJ

Telephone: +44 (0)1442 230589
Facsimile: +44 (0)1442 259232

Email: enquiries@ukla.org.uk
Website: www.ukla.org.uk

Executive Director: Rod Parker

Mark Hebblewhite

Douglas
Isle of Man

27th July 2005

Dear Mr. Hebblewhite,

Thank you for your letter of 17th July 2005 regarding your predicament with a cat flap.

If the problem still exists, I suggest you use a medical quality petroleum jelly, which will not be harmful to either yourself or Little Pea.

Kind regards

Yours sincerely,

R.G. Parker
Executive Director

A Company Limited By Guarantee
Registered in England No. 936857.
Registered Office: 34 Marlborough Road,
Chelmsford, Essex CM2 0JR.
VAT Reg. No. GB 240 8376 65

Mark Hebblewhite
Belmont Hill
Douglas
Isle of Man

United Kingdom Lubricants Association Ltd
Berkhamsted House
121 High Street
Berkhamsted
Herts
United Kingdom
HP4 2DJ

1st August 2005

Dear Mr Parker

Thank you for your letter dated 27th July. I am pleased to report that
following your expert advice I am now free of the cat-flap/pet entry
system that I was installing. Furthermore, it is working a treat and
Little Pea is now able to come and go as she pleases. I must say that
I expect she will be difficult to pick up for a few days, due to the
residue of petroleum jelly on her fur; holding her is very similar to
wrestling an eel.

Due to your kindness and swift response I now find myself drawn
to the world of lubricants and I was wondering if you have any job
vacancies at the moment. I adapt very easily to new situations and I
am able to learn new skills very quickly. I am extremely proficient at
listing things which I am sure is a bonus in any role in the lubricant
industry. My top 5 favourite birds of prey are as follows.

In reverse order
5) Snowy owl
4) Peregrine falcon
3) Eagle
2) Hawk
1) Buzzard (due to its curved yet pointy beak)

My hobbies include playing the trombone and putting things in
alphabetical order.

I look forward to your response, details of any vacancies and a top 5 list of your choosing.

Kind regards

Mark Hebblewhite.

Mark Hebblewhite

Mark Hebblewhite
Belmont Hill
Douglas
Isle of Man

McVitie's Consumer Services Department
PO Box 7249
Ashby de la Zouch
Leicestershire
LE65 2ZH

17th July 2005

Dear Sir or Madam

I would be most grateful if you could assist me in resolving a dispute that has arisen between myself and a gentleman whom I have recently met in the 24-hour garage.

My favourite accompaniment to a hot beverage has always been a custard cream in light of its delicate texture and sumptuous filling. However, the above mentioned gentleman says that a custard cream is nothing more than an albino Bourbon (his words). So how can you help me?

Flavourings aside, what is the difference in the manufacturing process between custard creams and Bourbons (or poor man's Penguins as I call them)?

I await your response.

Yours sincerely

Mark Hebblewhite.

Mark Hebblewhite

Mr Mark Hebblewhite

Douglas
Isle of Man

Our Ref : E046391DT   28th July 2005

Dear Mr Hebblewhite

Thank you for your letter dated 17th July 2005, in which you enquire about the
process of manufacture for Custard Creams and Bourbons.

The process of manufacture for both products is very similar. However, the Bourbon
biscuit shell is harder than that of the Custard Cream and the shells have granulated
sugar sprinkled on them.

The distinctive difference in flavour is that the Bourbon biscuit has chocolate
flavoured filling.

We hope this information is of help to you.

Yours sincerely

Mrs Diane Tunstall
Consumer Services Co-Ordinator

McVitie's Consumer Services Department, PO Box 7249,
Ashby-de-la-Zouch, Leicestershire LE65 2ZH
T UK 0500 011710 **T EIRE** 1800 409317 **F** 01530 411888
E mcvities.consumerservices@unitedbiscuits.com

McVitie's is part of
United Biscuits (UK) Limited.
Registered in England No. 2506007.
Registered Office: Hayes Park,
Hayes End Road, Hayes,
Middlesex UB4 8EE.

Mark Hebblewhite
Belmont Hill
Douglas
Isle of Man

Mrs Diane Tunstall
McVitie's Consumer Services Department
PO Box 7249
Ashby de la Zouch
Leicestershire
LE65 2ZH

Ref E046391DT

30th July 2005

Dear Diane

Thank you for your prompt response to my letter dated 17th July. I am most impressed by the efficiency of both yourself and your organisation and this being the case I have upped my biscuit consumption considerably as a mark of respect, whilst my consumption of your rivals' products has now dipped in my household to an unprecedented low. I am of course referring to Tunnock's teacakes.

By way of thanks I would like to visit your organisation with my collection of 'misshapes' that I have amassed over the years (including a rare 'sports biscuit' where the character appears to be playing the trombone) and give a brief talk and slide show to all interested parties. I would be grateful if you could ask around and get back to me with a projected estimate for the number of interested parties and if possible a proposed venue and time. I can assure you it will make a very interesting afternoon.

Yours faithfully

Mark Hebblewhite.

Mark Hebblewhite

Mr Mark Hebblewhite

Douglas
Isle of Man

Our Ref : e046391DT   4th August 2005

Dear Mr Hebblewhite

Thank you for your letter in which you kindly offer to visit our organisation to give a
brief talk and slideshow about your collection of 'misshapes'.

Unfortunately, on this occasion we are unable to accept your kind offer.

Yours sincerely

Mrs Diane Tunstall
Consumer Services Co-Ordinator

McVitie's Consumer Services Department, PO Box 7249,
Ashby-de-la-Zouch, Leicestershire LE65 2ZH
T UK 0500 011710 **T EIRE** 1800 409317 **F** 01530 411888
E mcvities.consumerservices@unitedbiscuits.com

McVitie's is part of
United Biscuits (UK) Limited
Registered in England No. 2506007
Registered Office: Hayes Park,
Hayes End Road, Hayes,
Middlesex UB4 8EE.

Mark Hebblewhite
Belmont Hill
Douglas
Isle of Man

Diane Tunstall
McVitie's Consumer Services Department
PO Box 7249
Ashby de la Zouch
Leicestershire
LE65 2ZH

6th August 2005

Dear Diane

I am most disappointed that there is insufficient demand amongst the staff for my 'misshapes' slide show. Are you sure you asked everyone in the office in your survey, including the part-timers? On a brighter note, I have noted that your efficiency is second to none in the biscuit customer service world. I do hope your superiors appreciate you. I have thought long and hard about how to reward you and your company for your assistance and I have settled on providing you with a top 5 list of my favourite animals that you may encounter during a walk in the mountains.

In reverse order

5) Brown bear
4) Wolf
3) Mountain goat
2) Elk
1) Cougar (or mountain lion)

It is very unlikely you will ever encounter a cougar but should this be the case the best way to get rid of it is to open your coat as wide as you can by holding on to the hem at the bottom. In this way you can appear bigger than you actually are thus frightening off the beast. This technique does not work with

brown bears in which case you should just run as fast as you can.
I look forward to a top 5 list of your choosing.

Many thanks

Mark Hebblewhite.

Mark Hebblewhite

Mr Mark Hebblewhite

Douglas
Isle of Man

Our Ref : E046391DT   10th August 2005

Dear Mr Hebblewhite

Thank you for your further letter. I am sorry to hear of your disappointment at us not being able to take you up on your offer of the slideshow.

Thank you, however, for your advise on how to deal with an encounter with a cougar or a brown bear.

I have passed this information on to my colleagues should they ever me stranded in the wilderness.

Yours sincerely

Mrs Diane Tunstall
Consumer Services Co-Ordinator

 PENGUIN Jaffa Cakes

McVitie's Consumer Services Department, PO Box 7249,
Ashby-de-la-Zouch, Leicestershire LE65 2ZH
T UK 0500 011710 **T EIRE** 1800 409317 **F** 01530 411888
E mcvities.consumerservices@unitedbiscuits.com

McVitie's is part of
United Biscuits (UK) Limited.
Registered in England No. 2506007
Registered Office: Hayes Park.
Hayes End Road, Hayes,
Middlesex UB4 8EE.

Mark Hebblewhite
Belmont Hill
Douglas
Isle of Man

Mrs Diane Tunstall
McVitie's Consumer Services Department
PO Box 7249
Ashby de la Zouch
Leicestershire
LE65 2ZH

12th August 2005

Ref E046391DT

Dear Diane

Once again thank you for your reply to my letter dated 6th August. Again I have noted the efficiency of your organisation and yourself and I do hope it makes you proud to know that I have plotted the swift responses to my letters onto a graph which I have positioned above my fruit bowl. I admire this on a daily basis (the graph not my fruit bowl). I appreciate your concern regarding your rejection of my slide show idea but I am most proud to announce I have got over it.

With regard to my advice on the best way to deal with an angry brown bear I have done some further research on the subject and I regret to inform you that the technique I described to you only applies to black bears. When encountering a brown bear you should simply play dead. I would be most grateful if you could pass on this change of instructions to your colleagues in case of emergency. This week I have been mostly engaged in tidying up the garden as I have a week off work but as I was mending the strimmer I had a flash of inspiration. Some time ago I watched a programme on TV about the famous psychic Uri Geller. Perhaps yourself and your colleagues would endeavour to assist me in an experiment I hope to conduct on Tuesday 16th August at 11.08 am after I have had my breakfast (Alpen). At this time exactly (11.08) I would like you all to focus your energy and thoughts and concentrate on attempting to influence my wife's thought processes by silently encouraging her to let me go out for a drink with my friends more often.

I do fully understand if you are not able to assist (although it would be appreciated), in which case a letter to my wife would suffice. Should you decide upon the second option I would be eternally grateful if you could outline that I only went out once on my own this month (to play snooker with Craig, Bob and Neil) and that it is very rare that I have ever lost money playing pool in the past. In addition to this I have washed up every day this week, cleaned the cat's litter tray twice, and have used Mr Muscle in the oven without damaging the rubber seal around the perimeter of the door. Many thanks in anticipation of your assistance with this endeavour and I hope to hear from you soon.

Yours faithfully

Mark Hebblewhite.

Mark Hebblewhite

Mark Hebblewhite
Belmont Hill
Douglas
Isle of Man

Office for National Statistics
Customer Contact Centre
Room 1015
Cardiff Road
Newport
NP10 8XG

17th July 2005

Dear Sir or Madam

As the home of official UK statistics I understand your organisation is used for data collation and research purposes and to that end I am writing to provide you with the following statistics which you may or may not already hold on your database. During the last 12 months (from 15th July 2004 to 15th July 2005) I have consumed a total of 300 cheese sandwiches broken down into sub-groups as follows.

Traditional Cheeses 160
Soft Cheese 70
International Cheese 50
Territorial / Speciality 15
Unclassifiable 5

These may be further split into sub-groups. (those with Branston Pickle accompaniment are in bold type)

Traditional Cheese	**Soft Cheese**	**International**
Mature Cheddar **40**	Brie 14	Mozzarella (ball) 30
Medium Mature	Camembert 12	Mozzarella (grated) **12**
Cheddar 32	Danish Blue **30**	Parmesan 10
Crumbly	Feta 4	Edam 19
Lancashire 18	Le Roulé 6	
Red Leicester **25**		
Double Gloucester **36**		

Territorial / Speciality   **Unclassifiable**

IOM Cracked Black Pepper **7**   Dairylea **5**

Saint Agur 8

155 sandwiches were accompanied by Mr Branston's famous pickle, a mighty 51.5%.

As you can see the most popular option falls into the traditional cheese category, accounting for 53% of total consumption, the most popular sub option being Mature Cheddar, accounting for 25% of traditional cheese consumption and a massive 13% of all cheese consumed.

The least consumed group (disregarding unclassifiable) being Territorial with only 5% of consumption.

The least popular choice from all groups is Feta with only 5.7% of total soft cheese consumption and a very poor 1.3% of all cheese consumed due to the fact it is too crumbly and goes off quickly. I would be very interested to see how these stats compare to the average UK male/female during the same period.

I do hope my research is of some use to you and I look forward to your response.

Yours sincerely

Mark Hebblewhite.

Mark Hebblewhite

Mark Hebblewhite
Belmont Hill
Douglas
Isle of Man

Department for Environment, Food and Rural Affairs
Room 231
Foss House
King's Pool
1-2 Peasholme Green
York
YO1 7PX

28th July 2005

Dear Sir or Madam

I have been given your address by National Statistics in Cardiff who said that you would be very interested in the research I have been undertaking into cheese over the last year or so. I enclose a copy of my letter to National Statistics and I look forward to your response.

Yours sincerely

Mark Hebblewhite.

Mark Hebblewhite

FCAFRD4, Food Statistics Branch, Area 146, Foss House,
King's Pool, 1-2 Peasholme Green,
York YO1 7PX

Telephone 01904 451000
Website www.defra.gov.uk

Department for Environment
Food and Rural Affairs

Mr. Mark Hepplewhite

Douglas
Isle of Man

Our ref 85/2005
Date 03/08/2005

Dear Mr. Hepplewhite

Cheese Statistics

Thank you for your letter that has been passed to me for reply.

I'm sorry to have to inform you that the statistics you so kindly supplied to my colleagues in
the Office for National Statistics are not acceptable for the purposes of the Family Food
Survey. We cannot accept unsolicited data.

If you are interested in food statistics and you have access to the Internet, then I
recommend you look at our website:

http://statistics.defra.gov.uk/esg/publications/efs/default.asp

There you can find an online version of the current Family Food report, and copies of
reports from previous years.

Thank you for your interest.

Yours sincerely

Andrew M Scaife
Administrative Officer

Direct Line 01904 455303 **GTN** 5137 5303
Fax 01904 455254
Email andrew.scaife@defra.gsi.gov.uk

INVESTOR IN PEOPLE

Mark Hebblewhite
Belmont Hill
Douglas
Isle of Man

Andrew Scaife
Department for Environment, Food and Rural Affairs
Food Statistics Branch
Area 146
Foss House
King's Pool
1-2 Peasholme Green
York
YO1 7PX

9th August 2005

Ref Cheese Statistics

Dear Andrew

Thank you for your reply to my letter dated 28th July. I understand your disappointment in not being able to use my cheese statistics as they are not solicited – however, I think I may have found a way around the problem. In order to authenticate my data I can send you some drawings my wife made of me whilst I was consuming the sandwiches in question. She is a courtroom artist by trade so they really are very lifelike. The only problem I can foresee is that due to their similar colour it is difficult to tell the difference on the drawings between Red Leicester and Mature Cheddar so I suppose you would have to take my word for it. I look forward to your response and I am happy to supply details of other projects I am carrying out should you be interested.

Yours faithfully

Mark Hebblewhite.

Mark Hebblewhite

Mark Hebblewhite
Belmont Hill
Douglas
Isle of Man

Thomas Tunnock Ltd
34 Old Mill Road
Uddingston
Glasgow
G71 7HH

20th July 2005

Dear Sir

I am writing to let you know how much I enjoy your products, in particular the caramel logs which I consume on a daily basis. Over the years and especially since my retirement they have proved to be something of a lifeline to me. I have been told that you can set a clock by my habit of a cup of tea and a caramel log or teacake at 2pm! Myself and my friend Neil regularly share your products over a hot drink and a good chat. Please keep up the good work. On a final note I have been inspired to compose a short verse which I do hope you will take pleasure from. Better still, should you think it worthy I would very much like to assist your company in any future marketing campaign should you desire it. Please advise me whether you would like my assistance.

It's nearly 2 o'clock my friend
And each and every day
A light and crunchy treat
So sweet
To pass the time away

Made on the Old Mill Road
My friend
Steadfast, as if to show
They've been around a long long time
Whilst others come and go

A wafer strong and angular
Surely the choice of men
Savour
Flavour
Bite by bite
It's Tunnock's time again.

Once again keep up the good work!

Yours sincerely

Mark Hebblewhite.

Mark Hebblewhite

CHOCOLATE BISCUIT MANUFACTURER

34 OLD MILL ROAD
UDDINGSTON
GLASGOW G71 7HH
TELEPHONE: 01698 813551
FAX NO: 01698 815691
REGISTERED NUMBER 28747 SCOTLAND
EXPORT DEPARTMENT
DIRECT FAX LINE: 01698 815931
E-MAIL: sales@tunnock.co.uk

ABT/MP

26 July 2005

Mark Hebblewhite

Douglas
ISLE OF MAN

Dear Mr Hebblewhite

Many thanks for your letter and of your interest in our products. We appreciate this
very much. Thank you also for your verse and we shall keep your offer of assistance
in mind.

Please accept this crystal glass as a keepsake.

Yours sincerely

A Boyd Tunnock CBE
(Managing Director)

Encl. 1 glass

SOUTHERN OFFICE: BISHOP HOUSE NORTH,
BATH ROAD, TAPLOW NR MAIDENHEAD, BERKSHIRE, SL6 0NY
TELEPHONE: 01628 666080   FAX: 01628 666070

Certificate No. FM 29790

Mark Hebblewhite
Belmont Hill
Douglas
Isle of Man

Mr A Boyd Tunnock CBE
Thomas Tunnock Ltd
34 Old Mill Road
Uddingston
Glasgow
G71 7HH

1st August 2005

Dear Mr Tunnock

Thank you so much for your letter and the Edinburgh crystal. It was such a pleasant surprise to receive it and it really made my day. I am most flattered to accept your offer of assisting the company with its marketing campaigns and, furthermore, I am pleased to say that thanks to your kindness all my work will be provided absolutely free of any charge whatsoever. In addition to this nothing could make me happier than to become the company's official poet in residence (I am of course assuming that the post is not already occupied). Although I have had a number of my poems published, nothing would cheer me up more than having my poem published in your company's newsletter, a copy of which I would love to receive. Once again many thanks for your gift, which I felt was an extremely touching gesture from a large company such as yourselves.

I look forward to your reply.

Yours faithfully

Mark Hebblewhite.

Mark Hebblewhite

Mark Hebblewhite
Belmont Hill
Douglas
Isle of Man

Steve Gerrish
Events and Information
Resource Manager
British Potato Council
4300 Nash Court
John Smith Drive
Oxford Business Park
Oxford
OX4 2RT

23rd July 2005

Dear Steve

On September 15th this year I am hosting the world's first 'vegetable Olympics' event and I would very much like to invite you or a member of your organisation to attend as a competitor. I have secured attendance from members of all growing organisations and associations except representatives from the potato and turnip worlds. The day itself will be split into 10 activities with representatives from each of the vegetable associations competing against each other in all events, in all cases the traditional piece of sporting equipment used is to be substituted for the appropriate vegetable. It is hoped that the event will generate a great deal of positive press for all those organisations involved as well as being a fun day for all concerned.

Programme of events (all timings are approximate)

10:00-Opening speech, local and national radio link, and competitor photographs
10:20-Asparagus darts (round the clock)
10:40-Potato shot put
11:00-Turnip crown green bowls
11:20-800m carrot relay race (using carrot batons)
11:40-The hammer (using a bendy leak combined with a potato)

12:00-Lunch
13:00-Round up of scores
13:20-Rhubarb javelin
13:40-Flat mushroom discus
14:00-Cauliflower weightlifting (using full cases)
14:20-Pea shooting
14:40-Aubergine 'speedball' boxing
15:00-Round-up of scores and presentation of medals (broadcast live – local TV)

I do hope you are able to participate in this event and I look forward to your response.

Yours faithfully

Mark Hebblewhite.

Mark Hebblewhite

BRITISH POTATO COUNCIL

4300 Nash Court, John Smith Drive, Oxford Business Park South, Oxford OX4 2RT

Mark Hebblewhite

Douglas
Isle of Man

28 July 2005

Dear Mr Hebblewhite

Thank you for your kind invitation, to what sounds like a fantastic day, unfortunately on this occasion we will have to decline your offer due to other commitments.

Good luck with the event and hope everything goes well

Kind regards

Sue Lawton
BPC Marketing

Mark Hebblewhite
Belmont Hill
Douglas
Isle of Man

Sue Lawton
British Potato Council
4300 Nash Court
John Smith Drive
Oxford Business Park
Oxford
OX4 2RT

2nd August 2005

Dear Sue

I am sorry to have called you Steve in my previous letter but at least I got the first letter right.

Thank you for your prompt response to my letter dated 23rd July. I regret that you will not be able to attend due to other commitments but I understand that you are very busy and I have to consider the possibility that I should have given you a little more notice. I have a dilemma in that due to the event drawing closer and closer I had the competitor T-shirts printed last week which unfortunately feature your organisation's logo along with that of the other growing and marketing organisations who are taking part. I really should have waited until I had a definite 'yes' from yourselves. Would it still be possible to use the logo on this occasion or should I save the T-shirts in anticipation of your attendance at the Olympics next year? Another possibility is that I could use a friend to take part on your behalf and pretend he was a member of the Potato Council. I would make sure he would be well briefed and create a 'cover' for him so as to not to arouse the suspicions of the other competitors. The friend I have in mind is a semi professional athlete and there is a fairly good chance he could win the event thus gaining a little kudos for your organisation. Would you please let me know your thoughts on my plan in time to organise the briefing session with your 'attendee'.

I can assure you it will be our secret, I could even put a bet on for you.

Yours faithfully

Mark Hebblewhite.

Mark Hebblewhite

Mark Hebblewhite
Belmont Hill
Douglas
Isle of Man

British Activity Holiday Association
Morritt House
58 Station Approach
South Ruislip
HA4 6SA

28th July 2005

Dear Sir or Madam

My wife and I would like to ask your assistance in finding our dream holiday if you would be so kind as to help us. We have both enjoyed collecting Smurfs and engaging them in mock battles for some time now. We have been looking for something similar to the Lord of the Rings type themed holidays except with Smurfs so we can meet up with fellow enthusiasts for a weekend, ideally somewhere rural with tea and coffee-making facilities. Many thanks in anticipation of your help with this matter.

Yours sincerely

Mark Hebblewhite.

Mark Hebblewhite

BRITISH ACTIVITY HOLIDAY ASSOCIATION LTD

MORRITT HOUSE
58 STATION APPROACH
SOUTH RUISLIP
RUISLIP
HA4 6SA
tel: 020 8842 1292
fax: 020 8842 0090
email: info@baha.org.uk
web: www.baha.org.uk

Company No. 2508344

8th August 2005

Mark Hebblewhite

Douglas
Isle of Man

Dear Mr Hebblewhite,

Thank you for your letter of the 28th July. BAHA is the trade association for outdoor activity centres and summer camps. I regret to advise you that we have no information relating to holidays involving smurfs or Lord of the Rings type themed programmes. I'm not sure who to refer you to, but you could try contacting VisitEngland in London.

I hope you have better luck with your enquiries elsewhere.

Yours sincerely,

Martin Hudson
Chairman

Striving for Quality and Safety in the Activity Industry

Mark Hebblewhite
Belmont Hill
Douglas
Isle of Man

Martin Hudson
Chairman
British Activity Holiday Association
Morritt House
58 Station Approach
South Ruislip
Ruislip
HA4 6SA

11th August 2005

Dear Martin

Many thanks for your reply to my letter dated 28th July in which I enquired about 'smurf' themed holidays. Many thanks also for your suggestion to contact 'VisitEngland' in London. As a beekeeper by trade I appreciate the volume of letters you receive about holiday enquiries but I would like to trouble you with one more request. I have misplaced your original letter and my wife has accused me of not writing to you in the first place. Please would it be possible to give her a call or write to her suggesting some alternative holidays in order to appease her? We also enjoy orienteering and monkeys.

Yours faithfully

Mark Hebblewhite.

Mark Hebblewhite

Mark Hebblewhite
Belmont Hill
Douglas
Isle of Man

John Betteley
Lincoln Branch
British Cactus and Succulent Society
Holy Cross Church Hall
Skellingthorpe Road
Lincoln

28th July 2005

Dear John

I am writing to ask for your advice as I am from Lincoln originally and I still retain strong links with the city. I would like to know the best way to grow a cactus that would look nice on a window sill or next to the sink. If you could advise me which cactus will grow best in these locations I would be very grateful.

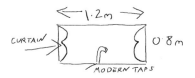

The window above the sink is the same size as the other one but the other way round. As you can see the maximum height is 0.8 metres. Also I would like to grow one that is not too spiky so I can open the window easily.

I look forward to your response.

Yours faithfully

Mark Hebblewhite.

Mark Hebblewhite

72

25 Old Hall Gardens,
Coddington, Newark,
Notts, NG 24 2QJ.

Dear Mark,

Your letter has been re directed to me as secretary of Lincoln Branch of the Cactus Society.

Ideally you need a sunny south-facing window and to turn the cacti around occasionally so that all sides have the sun. ~~Grow them in plastic saucer~~ Put the pots into plastic saucers so that you can water from below. Rainwater is best, and a low nitrogen feed (suitable for tomatoes). Water between March and the end of September. If the room is warm in winter, give them a drop of water (but no feed) once a month. Suitable genera are the less spiny forms of Mammillaria, rebutia, Sulcorebutia and Gymnocalycium. In fact most rebutias & sulcorebutias have only fine spines and are more likely to flower.

Regards. John Betteley

Mark Hebblewhite
Belmont Hill
Douglas
Isle of Man

John Betteley
Secretary
Lincoln Branch
British Cactus and Succulent Society
25 Old Hall Gardens
Coddington
Newark
Notts
NG24 2QJ

16th August 2005

Dear John

Many thanks for your letter in response to my cactus enquiry. I have noted your new address since my previous letter was addressed incorrectly, I trust the move went well. I have just moved house and all my mugs were smashed. I have just purchased some Gymnocalycium and a Sulcorebutia (cactus) and they look lovely on my window sill. Many thanks for the advice. I have given my succulent some nitrogen feed as you recommended but after a couple of days the tomatoes that you suggested I put in the saucer around the base of the cactus have started to wither. Do you think that this is because of the sun's heat or perhaps I am not feeding the Gymnocalycium enough and it is taking the tomatoes' energy? Once again many thanks for your advice and I hope to hear from you soon.

Yours faithfully

Mark Hebblewhite.

Mark Hebblewhite

25 Old Hall Gdns,
Coddington, Newark
Notts NG 24 2QJ.

Dear Mark

Thanks for your letter of 16th Aug.
You feed the plants with a low nitrogen food
such as 'Tomorite' (diluted to the recommended
strength on the bottle).

You do not have to put tomatoes around
the saucer — just use a tomato feed
such as TOMORITE.

Sorry for the apparent confusion.

John Betteley

Mark Hebblewhite
Belmont Hill
Douglas
Isle of Man

John Betteley
25 Old Hall Gardens
Coddington
Newark
NG24 2QJ

25th August 2005

Dear John

Thank you for your letter about my cactuses. I have taken the tomatoes away from the saucer and bought some TOMORITE from B and Q. They (the cactuses) look nicer now without the tomatoes spoiling them.

Please can you tell me what is the difference between a cactus and a succulent? I have been told that they are just about the same but succulents are albinos. Also does the Lincoln Cactus and Succulent Society have any mugs for sale or T-shirts? Also how do I join if that is possible? I am quite proud now I have got my first cactuses and I would like a T-shirt or a mug as a talking point when visitors come to my house. As I said in my previous letter all my mugs were smashed when I moved house. Perhaps I could start a branch in the Isle of Man or we could have a joint Lincoln and Isle of Man club for people that live in both places such as myself. I would appreciate your thoughts on this. Now I have started my cactuses hobby I am giving up collecting batteries. If you would like any please just give me the size you require, e.g. AA.

Many thanks for your help and I hope to hear from you soon.

Yours faithfully

Mark Hebblewhite.

Mark Hebblewhite

Mark Hebblewhite
Belmont Hill
Douglas
Isle of Man

The British Association of Barbershop Singers
Clifton House
Rickards
Whittlesford
Cambridge
CB2 4YT

28th July 2005

Dear Sir or Madam

I am writing to ask for your help in expanding my wife's sticker collection. Would it be possible to purchase some from your organisation (round ones if possible)? The most prized ones feature artists and/or commemorative dates. Many thanks for your help with this matter.

Yours sincerely

Mark Hebblewhite.

Mark Hebblewhite

singbarbershop ○ com

THE BRITISH ASSOCIATION OF BARBERSHOP SINGERS
Reply to: Clifton House Rickards Whittlesford Cambridge CB2 4YT
Telephone: 01223 833063

Dear Mr Hebblewhite, Thanks for your letter but we do not have BABS stickers and so I am unable to help you.

With Compliments

David Wright 08/08/06

Mark Hebblewhite
Belmont Hill
Douglas
Isle of Man

David Wright
The British Association of Barbershop Singers
Clifton House
Rickards
Whittlesford
Cambridge
CB2 4YT

16th August 2005

Ref Stickers?

Dear David

Many thanks for your reply to my letter dated 28th July. It appears that there has been some misunderstanding in that I requested to purchase some programmes (of events) for my wife's collection. I can only assume I made some sort of typing error and I apologise for the confusion I may have inadvertently (accidentally) caused. Also are there any BABS (British Association of Barbershop Singers) associations on the Isle of Man as I would very much like to join? Please could you advise of the membership criteria and any medical (if applicable) that is undertaken prior to enrolment.

Yours faithfully

Mark Hebblewhite.

Mark Hebblewhite

singbarbershop ○ com

THE BRITISH ASSOCIATION OF BARBERSHOP SINGERS
Reply to: Clifton House Rickards Whittlesford Cambridge CB2 4YT
Telephone: 01223 833063

Mr Mark Hebblewhite

Douglas
Isle of Man

24th August 2005

Dear Mark,

Thank you for your letter of 16th August. I regret to have to tell you that we do not have any programmes of events as BABS is the umbrella organisation to which individual clubs belong and, as such we do not run events requiring 'programmes' as such.

With regard to your enquiry about BABS clubs, we do not have any member clubs in your locality unfortunately. If you have access to the internet the clubs are listed on our website at www,singbarbershop.com and indeed you will also find much other information about barbershop there too.

I am sorry that we are unable to be more help.

Yours sincerely

David M Wright

www.singbarbershop.com
Registered in England No 3823721 Registered Charity Ref. No: 1080930
Registered Office: Clifton House Rickards Whittlesford Cambridge CB2 4YT
General e-mail: ask@babsco.co.uk

Mark Hebblewhite
Belmont Hill
Douglas
Isle of Man

David Wright
The British Association of Barbershop Singers
Clifton House
Rickards
Whittlesford
Cambridge
CB2 4YT

29th August 2005

Dear David

Thank you for your letter dated 24th August. I am sorry to hear that BABS (British Association of Barbershop Singers) is an umbrella association. Both my wife and I were informed (unreliably it seems) that the organisation was solely concerned with group singing efforts. Perhaps the organisation should change its name to something more appropriate that reflects its dual purposes. Could I suggest 'The British Association of Umbrellas and Barbershop Singers'? I regret to inform you that I have no interest whatsoever in umbrellas but if you can advise me how I can train to become a barbershop singer I would be most grateful. Many thanks for your assistance.

Yours faithfully

Mark Hebblewhite.

Mark Hebblewhite

singbarbershop ○ com

THE BRITISH ASSOCIATION OF BARBERSHOP SINGERS
Reply to: Clifton House Rickards Whittlesford Cambridge CB2 4YT
Telephone: 01223 833063

Mr Mark Hebblewhite

Douglas
Isle of Man

13th September 2005

Dear Mark,

Re BABS clubs

Thank you for your letter of 29th August.

Unfortunately we do not have any member clubs, where you can learn to sing barbershop, on the Isle of Man. However If you access the internet the locations of our clubs are listed on our website at www,singbarbershop.com and from this you can see if there is a club location that might be of interest to you.

Additionally, each year, at the end of August, we run a two day residential event called Harmony College and this is expressly intended to help people, members and non-members, learn more about Barbershop singing. Details of this educational event, including what it covers how to enrol, cost etc. are published on our website, nearer the time. If you would like to receive details of Harmony College when they are available please let me know.

Yours sincerely

David Wright.

David M Wright

www.singbarbershop.com
Registered in England No 3823721 Registered Charity Ref. No: 1080930
Registered Office: Clifton House Rickards Whittlesford Cambridge CB2 4YT
General e-mail: ask@babsco.co.uk

Mark Hebblewhite
Belmont Hill
Douglas
Isle of Man

David Wright
The British Association of Barbershop Singers
Clifton House
Rickards
Whittlesford
Cambridge
CB2 4YT

27th September 2005

Dear Dave

Thanks for your letter dated 13th September. I have had a look at the BABS website you mentioned in your letter and I am most excited. It looks like I have missed my chance to go to the Harmony college this year but it would be great if you could let me know the details for next year i.e. price, location, menu etc. As I am new to the hobby would it be possible to come along to one of your meetings in order to get an idea of what goes on? My wife and I would also like the chance to perform for you to see if we are up to scratch. My wife does an excellent version of 'Smoke on the water' accompanied by me on the bongos. We would very much like the chance for you to evaluate our performance.

Yours faithfully

Mark Hebblewhite.

Mark Hebblewhite

Mark Hebblewhite
Belmont Hill
Douglas
Isle of Man

Lord Faulkner
Royal Society for the Prevention of Accidents
Edgbaston Park
353 Bristol Road
Edgbaston
Birmingham
B5 7ST

29th July 2005

Dear Sir

In May of last year I experienced an unfortunate accident which may have been prevented had I had the foresight to read the label on a can of deodorant I was disposing of. I have a large garden and in the rear left-hand corner I regularly have bonfires in the summer months to dispose of garden refuse etc. For some unknown reason on July 12th last year the bin men did not arrive so I took it on myself to dispose of the week's rubbish on the bonfire. Unknown to me was the fact that there were a number of aerosol cans contained in this rubbish, one of which when burnt gave a whoosh type noise which I found curious. On closer inspection a second can exploded with enough force to blow the top off a nearby cactus which my late grandfather gave to me as a holiday memento from his trip to Poland.

I would like to ask if you are currently running any propellant safety courses as I would very much like to attend one with the aim of using my new knowledge to educate people about the dangers of incorrect disposal of aerosols. I have already approached my local college of adult education with regard to running an aerosol safety course and their response has been promising, providing I can provide proof of a recognised qualification. Hence I would very much like to attend the above mentioned course and I would be grateful if you could provide me with details of how to apply together with information on the fees payable.

Thank you in anticipation.

Yours sincerely

Mark Hebblewhite.

Mark Hebblewhite

RoSPA House, Edgbaston Park
353 Bristol Road, Birmingham B5 7ST
Tel: +44 (0) 870 777 2171/0121 248 2000
Fax: +44 (0) 870 777 2199/0121 248 2001
www.rospa.com
Patron: Her Majesty The Queen

Mr Mark Hebblewhite

Douglas
Isle of Man

9th August 2005

Dear Mr Hebblewhite

Training courses

Thank you for your letter of 29th July addressed to Lord Faulkner. I am sorry to hear of your experience when trying to dispose of your rubbish. We have conducted a publicity campaign in the past on aerosol dangers sponsored by the British Aerosol Manufacturers' Association. I enclose a copy of the leaflet produced.

I'm afraid we don't have the resources to run any courses on aerosol safety. Details of the courses we do run can be found on our website at www.rospa.com

Yours sincerely

Sarah Colles
Home Safety Adviser

One of the world's leading safety organisations, serving all areas of Occupational and Public Safety

Registered Charity No. 207823 and a company limited by guarantee registered in England, No. 231435
Registered Office: RoSPA House, Edgbaston Park, 353 Bristol Road, Birmingham B5 7ST

INVESTOR IN PEOPLE

Mark Hebblewhite
Belmont Hill
Douglas
Isle of Man

Sarah Colles
Royal Society for the Prevention of Accidents
ROSPA House
Edgbaston Park
353 Bristol Road
Birmingham
B5 7ST

17th August 2005

Dear Sarah

Thank you for your letter dated 9th August in response to my letter dated 29th July which was addressed to Lord Faulkner whom I mistakenly believed was in charge of your organisation. Can I assume as a representative of the organisation you are also a member of the nobility? Many thanks for the informative leaflet and I only wish I had read it prior to my unfortunate accident. I am pleased to inform you that despite my lack of aerosol safety qualifications I intend to do my bit to educate the public about these dangerous articles by dressing up as a can of shaving foam and handing out copies of the flyer in my immediate neighbourhood. Please would it be possible for you to supply some stickers to assist with my endeavours. I intend to undertake this activity on 15th September and would be extremely grateful for your support. Also would it be possible to come on a course of your choice free of charge in light of my commitment? I once got a suitcase attached to my foot by accident and had to go to hospital.

Yours faithfully

Mark Hebblewhite.

Mark Hebblewhite

Mark Hebblewhite
Belmont Hill
Douglas
Isle of Man

King's Lynn Scale Model Club
10 Mannington Place
South Wootton
King's Lynn
Norfolk
PE30 3UD

2nd August 2005

Dear Sir or Madam

I am a former resident of King's Lynn and I have been making models since my retirement for over 6 years now. I would very much like to join your club but I am not sure if I am eligible as although I am often in the area I am no longer a resident. To date I have constructed 6 models of buildings in the King's Lynn area, my latest being a scale model of Greyfriars Tower which I have recently completed after 4 months' work. I would be grateful if I could bring this along to one of your meetings as I am most proud of it, having spent so much time and effort on it. Whilst my previous models have been constructed of more traditional materials, this particular one is unique in that it is constructed entirely of a mix of pasta bound together with egg white. I would very much appreciate the opportunity to show you my work and the techniques that I have used. I look forward to your response.

Yours sincerely

Mark Hebblewhite.

Mark Hebblewhite

KING'S LYNN
SCALE MODEL CLUB

10 Mannington Place, South Wootton, King's Lynn, Norfolk, PE30 3UD, UK
Telephone: 01553 673744   E-Mail: paint.by.post@klmatrix.co.uk

10 August 2005

Douglas
Isle of Man

Dear Mark

Thank you for your letter dated 2 august 2005. You will be most welcome to come along to our meetings. They are held on the second and fourth Wednesday of every month, in the first floor meeting room of the workers club, in church street King's Lynn.

August: 10 – 24
September: 14 – 28
October: 12 – 26
November: 9 – 23
December: 7 – 21?

Regards

David Crump

David Crump

Mark Hebblewhite
Belmont Hill
Douglas
Isle of Man

David Crump
King's Lynn Scale Model Club
10 Mannington Place
South Wootton
King's Lynn
Norfolk
PE30 3UD

16th August 2005

Dear Mr Crump

Thank you for your letter dated 10th August. I am thrilled that you have invited me to your meeting to display my model of Greyfriars Tower. I hope to attend on the 28th September with my wife if that is possible. Without being presumptuous, please could you forward details of the induction and dress code for the event. I would very much like to wear my V-neck jumper and slacks but my wife says they would be too casual. Once again thank you for your letter and I look forward to meeting with you and my fellow members soon.

Yours faithfully

Mark Hebblewhite.

Mark Hebblewhite

KING'S LYNN
SCALE MODEL CLUB

10 Mannington Place, South Wootton, King's Lynn, Norfolk, PE30 3UD, UK
Telephone: 01553 673744   E-Mail: paint.by.post@klmatrix.co.uk

30 August 2005

Douglas
Isle of Man

Dear Mark

Thank you for your letter dated 16 August 2005. We do not have a dress
code; casual will be fine.
In my last letter I forgot to mention that the meetings start about 7:30pm
I have included a small map, and look forward to meeting you.

Regards

David Crump

David Crump

David Crump
10 Mannington Place
South Wootton
King's Lynn
Norfolk
PE30 3UD

7th September 2005

Dear Crump

Thank you for your letter dated 30th August. I am most relieved that the dress code for the society is not formal. Thank you also for the map as although we are frequent visitors to the area it never ceases to amaze me how much changes in so little time. Would it be possible for you to let me know if it would be possible to house my model of Greyfriars Tower in a refrigerator prior to the meeting on the 28th September? In warm weather the egg white binding can loosen and lead to subsidence. Also, in appreciation of my invitation to visit, I would like to show my gratitude to both yourself and the other members with the offer of access to my collection of batteries which I have put together over the last 12 years. Due to a surplus in my collection I now have a storage problem so if yourself or any members would like any free of charge please let me know the size and quantity required, e.g. PP9 x 16. I would be glad to assist in any battery shortfall your members may be experiencing.

Yours faithfully

Mark Hebblewhite.

Mark Hebblewhite

Mark Hebblewhite
Belmont Hill
Douglas
Isle of Man

Dr Ken Young
British Robot Association
International Manufacturing Centre
University of Warwick
Coventry
CV4 7AL

2nd August 2005

Dear Ken

Please could you advise me where I can get some new bits for my 'Big Trak'. One of the photon laser cannons is wonky and the trailer hoist mechanism has been broken after it crashed into the door frame whilst I was trying to deliver my dad an apple from behind the settee. As a fellow robot lover, can you help?

Yours faithfully

Mark Hebblewhite.

Mark Hebblewhite

Michelle Zhang
British Automation and Robot Association
International Manufacturing Center
University of Warwick
Coventry
CV4 7AL
Tel: 024 765 73742
Fax: 024 765 73743
Email: bara_a@wmgmail.wmg.warwick.ac.uk

Mark Hebblewhite

Douglas
Isle of Man

5 August 2005

Dear Mr. Hebblewhite,

Unfortunately, BARA does not have any specific company who manufacture the parts for 'Big Trak'. However, I found the following URLs by some 'Big Trak' fans like you. Maybe they will give you more hints.

- http://www.robotroom.com/BigTrak.html
- http://www.lavalamp.demon.co.uk/bigtrak/bigtrak.htm
- http://www.earthwidemoth.com/mt/archives/2004_11.html
- http://www.bugeyedmonster.com/toys/bigtrak/

I hope this will be of some help.

Best wishes,

Michelle

Michelle Zhang

Mark Hebblewhite
Belmont Hill
Douglas
Isle of Man

Michelle Zhang
British Robot and Automation Association
International Manufacturing Centre
University of Warwick
Coventry
CV4 7AL

9th August 2005

Dear Michelle

Many thanks for your letter in response to my letter dated 2nd August. I am very sorry to have called you Dr Ken in my last letter – this is because I have recently purchased a new computer and I have not got used to the keys yet. The links you provided me with were most helpful in terms of obtaining spares and so with any luck 'Big Trak' will be fully operational again soon. If Big Trak's battery were sufficiently powerful and there was not the considerable problem of the Irish sea I would programme Big Trak to deliver you a box of chocolates by way of thanks for your assistance. I would also be grateful if you could advise me of any applications your organisation may have developed that may be used to improve my machine in terms of better cannons and trailer manoeuvrability programmes etc. I would also be interested to learn a little more about your organisation and whether or not you possess any robots, Michelle. I am currently in the process of designing a robot for use in the beekeeping industry and I would be happy to share my design with you. Once again many thanks for your assistance and I hope to hear from you soon.

Yours faithfully

Mark Hebblewhite.

Mark Hebblewhite

Mark Hebblewhite
Belmont Hill
Douglas
Isle of Man

Philip Gibson
Dairy Farmers of Britain
Alpha Building
London Road
Stapeley
Nantwich
Cheshire
CW5 7JW

7th August 2005

Dear Philip

For a number of years my wife and I have been producing cheese on a very small scale and would very much like to market this on a purely local basis. A local shopkeeper has agreed to sell my product on the condition that all legal requirements are met. Please could you advise me of the regulations and legalities that would apply to an operation of this nature.

Your assistance in this matter would be greatly appreciated.

Yours sincerely

Mark Hebblewhite.

Mark Hebblewhite

Dairy Farmers of Britain °

August 16, 2005

Mark Hebblewhite

Douglas
Isle of Man

Dear Mark

Thank you for your letter of August 7 relating to your cheese manufacturing and retailing operations.

I am in no way an expert on the legal requirements relating to the activities you describe. However, I would advise that you contact the local environmental health department on the Isle of Man, who will be best placed to advise you on the relevant food safety issues. It would also be worth contacting a business insurance adviser regarding the liability insurances that you will require.

I wish you every success in your enterprise.

Yours sincerely

Philip Gibson
Head of PR

Head Office
Alpha Building, London Road, Stapeley, Nantwich, CW5 7JW
Tel: 08700 10 81 8 1   Fax: 08700 10 81 88
www.dairyfarmersofbritain.com

Mark Hebblewhite
Belmont Hill
Douglas
Isle of Man

Philip Gibson
Head of PR
Dairy Farmers of Britain
Head Office
Alpha Building
London Road
Stapeley
Nantwich
CW5 7JW

Ref Cheese production and retailing

20th August 2005

Dear Philip

Thank you for your reply to my letter dated 7th August. With regard to my cheese manufacturing operation I have contacted my local environmental health officer, as you suggested in your letter, with regard to food safety issues and legal requirements. However, to my disappointment he has informed me that their organisation would take a dim view if I were to attempt to sell my product through local retailers due to its unorthodox production methods and ingredients.

It would appear that for reasons I can fully understand Environmental Health would only sanction the retailing of cheese made in a more controlled environment than my small operation is capable of reaching. I must stress that my standards are most stringent, perhaps more so than many larger producers. In addition to this they have suggested that since cheese made from the milk of cats is not the norm in this country, they cannot vouch for its safety and quality 100%.

I am currently producing half a kilo per week and since I have more than enough for my own use and I am not allowed to sell it, I have decided to give my product away in the hope that it may stimulate a market. Would it be possible to provide you and your colleagues at the Dairy Farmers of Britain with a sample in order that you can judge the quality of the product yourselves? The finished product looks and tastes very similar to feta but is slightly more tangy. I would welcome your opinion on my product and I look forward to your response. Once again many thanks for your assistance.

Yours faithfully

Mark Hebblewhite.

Mark Hebblewhite

Mark Hebblewhite
Belmont Hill
Douglas
Isle of Man

Customer Services
ASDA House
Southbank
Great Wilson St
Leeds
LS11 5AD

7th August 2005

On 17th July I purchased a 750g box of Rice Crispies from your store in Leeds. I have enjoyed Rice Crispies for years as a satisfying breakfast but I was less than happy with my purchase on this occasion. As you will know Rice Crispies should contain 17% of the recommended daily amount of iron per 30g serving. My recently acquired box contains nothing like this quota.

As a result I have been moody, short tempered and less energetic than usual and this being the case I may switch to Sugar Puffs as a consequence of this nutritional shortfall unless you are able to provide a satisfactory explanation.

Yours sincerely

Mark Hebblewhite.

Mark Hebblewhite

part of the **WAL★MART** family

ASDA Stores Ltd
ASDA House
Southbank
Great Wilson Street
Leeds LS11 5AD
Tel: +44(0)113 243 5435
Fax: +44(0)113 241 8666
Minicom: 0800 068 3003
www.asda.com

Our Ref: 6205594

12/08/2005

Mr M Hebblewhite

DOUGLAS
ISLE OF MAN

Dear Mr Hebblewhite

Thank you for taking the time and trouble to let me know about the problem with the Rice Crispies that you bought from your local store.

It is very important to us that all ASDA brand products are of the highest quality and value. We work closely with our suppliers to thoroughly research and test products before they reach the shelves, so it is always disappointing when a product fails to satisfy one of our customers.

Your complaint is very important to us and I would like to assure you that each complaint is taken very seriously. Every week we produce reports for all business areas giving the reasons for customer returns. This information is then used to improve products and services.

All ASDA packaging contains unique codes that help us to identify both supplier and production details. If you still have the packaging, or have cause to complain about any other product in future, I would be very grateful if you could forward it to me at the above address or return it to your local store.

I hope you will accept my personal apologies that you were unhappy with this particular ASDA product, and that this incident will not deter you from enjoying our products in future. If I can be of any further assistance to you please do not hesitate to contact me.

Yours sincerely

Shabana Latif
ASDA Customer Relations

Registered in England No. 464777

Registered Office
ASDA House, Southbank
Great Wilson Street, Leeds LS11 5AD

BRITAIN'S NO.1 PLACE TO WORK
as voted by THE FINANCIAL TIMES 2003

Mark Hebblewhite
Belmont Hill
Douglas
Isle of Man

Shabana Latif
ASDA Customer Relations
ASDA House
Southbank
Great Wilson Street
Leeds
LS11 5AD

16th August 2005

Ref 6205594

Dear Shabana

Thank you for your letter dated 12th August. I am sorry that my previous letter was a little abrupt but I was understandably upset after my breakfast was ruined. I accept your personal apologies for my dissatisfaction with the product I purchased and I do hope you accept mine for the tone of my previous letter. I am afraid that I do not have the packaging for the product as I have shredded (cut up into small pieces) it to provide a nest for my kittens. Please can you advise whether there is any way I can take my complaint forward without the packaging. Also would it be possible to advise me whether or not ASDA sell proper cat baskets, the sort that can be hung on a radiator, ideally in yellow to match the cat's-eyes? Many thanks for your assistance with these matters.

Yours faithfully

Mark Hebblewhite.

Mark Hebblewhite

Mark Hebblewhite
Belmont Hill
Douglas
Isle of Man

Ted Sedman
The Handlebar Club
Windsor Castle Pub
Crawford Place
London

17th August 2005

Dear Ted

I do not have a moustache but I would very much like to join your club. Is it possible to join as an associate? If this is possible please could you forward details of how I can join. I very much enjoy raising money for charity and I feel that with the backing of your organisation I could up my collecting capacity considerably. I have only met one man with a handlebar moustache on the Isle of Man so I feel that membership would give me an edge with regard to individuality. Also does your organisation have a motto? If not I would like to suggest one that I hope you can use, which I feel is catchy and to the point.

'a man with a handlebar moustache can be relied upon in times of need because they are a symbol of individuality and as such demand respect from others'

Many thanks for your help with this matter and I hope to hear from you soon.

Yours faithfully

Mark Hebblewhite.

Mark Hebblewhite

President
Ted Sedman,
7 Mytchett Heath,
Mytchett,
CAMBERLEY,
Surrey. GU16 6DP
Tel. 01252 545432
ted@sedman.org

Secretary
Rod Littlewood,
560 Walton Road,
WEST MOLESEY,
Surrey. KT8 2EQ
Tel. 020 8941 6923
rod.littlewood@btinternet.com

The Handlebar Club

© 1947

www.handlebarclub.org.uk

Vice-President
Mike Solomons,
'Kyle Cottage',
39 High Street,
Findon Village,
West Sussex. BN14 0SU
Tel. 01903 877255
mike.solomons@ukgateway.net

Treasurer
Albert Tang
9E Logan Place
Kensington
LONDON W8 6QN
Tel. 020 7373 3401
alberttang@mac.com

23 August 2005

Dear Mark,

Thank you for your letter and for your interest in the Handlebar Club.

We do indeed have associate members of the Club. Anyone who supports the aims of the club but does not have the necessary qualification to become a full member, is welcome to become a "Friend of the Handlebar Club". The annual subscription is half of the full membership subscription, and so is currently £10. For this you will receive copies of the club newsletter which is published about four times a year. In addition you will be welcome at our regular "first Friday" meetings held at the Windsor Castle pub in London, and also to join us for the A.G.M. weekend (though friends are not eligible to vote at the A.G.M.). We also have a special tie for friends, which costs £10 (including postage). It bears the club logo on a blue background, and is distinct from the official club tie with its maroon background.

I enclose a copy of the relevant application form. Please do join - as far as I know, we have never previously had a member from the Isle of Man.

I assume that you do not have an e-mail address, but if it is possible for you to look on the internet, for example at a public library or an "internet café", then please take the opportunity to look at our web site at www.handlebarclub.org.uk where you will find a lot of background information about the Club and our activities.

With all good wishes

Yours sincerely

(Ted Sedman)

Mark Hebblewhite
Belmont Hill
Douglas
Isle of Man

Tiffany
25 Old Bond Street
London
W1S 4QB

18th August 2005

Dear Tiffany

I am writing because my daughter would very much like your autograph. She has been a fan since 1987's 'I think we're alone now'. It would make a great birthday present for her. Also, do you have any mugs with your face on them? I do hope you are able to help me with this.

Yours sincerely

Mark Hebblewhite.

Mark Hebblewhite

TIFFANY & CO.
25 OLD BOND STREET
LONDON W1S 4QB
TELEPHONE 020 7409 2790
FACSIMILE 020 7491 3110

Mark Hebblewhite

Douglas
Isle of Man

Wednesday 24th August 2005

Dear Mr Hebblewhite,

Thank you for your letter dated 18th August. I regret to inform you that you letter has reached Tiffany & Co., jewellery and speciality retailers, and that we are in no way affiliated with Tiffany the US recording artist.

I enclose a copy of our latest catalogue in case it is of interest to your daughter.

Yours sincerely

Jennifer Willows

TIFFANY & CO. REGISTERED IN ENGLAND NO. 1997250
REGISTERED VAT. NO. 445 973022

Mark Hebblewhite
Belmont Hill
Douglas
Isle of Man

Jennifer Willows
Tiffany and Co
25 Old Bond Street
London
W1S 4QB

29th August 2005

Dear Jennifer

Thank you for your letter dated 24th August. I can only apologise that I was supplied the incorrect information as regards the address for Tiffany (the US recording artist). Whilst I would very much like to purchase something from your catalogue for my daughter, what she really wants is Tiffany's autograph. It is her birthday on 9th September (she is 24). Please would it be possible to write to her and wish her happy birthday signing your name Tiffany? I think your headed paper would be enough to convince her that it was the real thing. I promised her this autograph for her birthday but I have been unsuccessful so far. I realise this is cheating a little but I think it will work. Many thanks for your help with this as it is my last chance.

Yours hopefully

Mark Hebblewhite.

Mark Hebblewhite

Mark Hebblewhite
Belmont Hill
Douglas
Isle of Man

Chris O' Keefe
Independent Betting Arbitration Service
PO Box 44781
London
SW1W 0WR

18th August 2005

Dear Chris

I recently held a crisp tasting evening with some friends (people I know) and I enclose a copy of the score sheet. There is some dispute over whether or not maize snacks should have been included. If this is the case because they are not real crisps I would have won hands down. Please can you advise me of your findings ASAP and forward the bill for your services to my wife.

Yours faithfully

Mark Hebblewhite.

Mark Hebblewhite

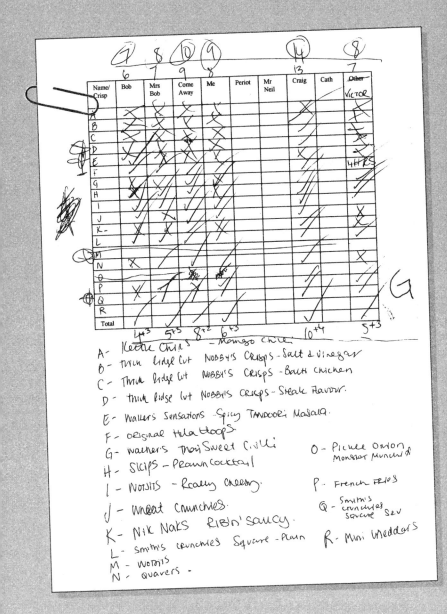

Mark Hebblewhite
Belmont Hill
Douglas
Isle of Man

Richard Branston
Branston Pickle Premier Foods
Premier House
Griffiths Way
St Albans
AL1 2RE

19th August 2005

Dear Richard

I am writing first and foremost to congratulate you on providing myself and my wife with the most satisfying sandwich filling. Over the years we have enjoyed your famous pickle in its variety of formats on an almost daily basis. We really are sandwich lovers and your magic recipe really does make a fantastic accompaniment. For your information I have enclosed a copy of my letter to the Office for National Statistics. As you can see 59.7% of the cheese I have consumed over the last year was accompanied by your pickle which really is a fantastic result for you. On a final note I would very much like to become the official Virgin statistician. I salute you my bearded friend.

Yours sincerely

Mark Hebblewhite.

Mark Hebblewhite

Please Quote Ref: E/024661/BS/07

7th September 2005

Mr M Hebblewhite

Douglas
Isle of Man

Dear Mr Hebblewhite

Thank you so much for your letter dated 19th August 2005, which we read with great interest, though I do have to report that we are not associated with Mr Richard Branson of the Virgin group of companies.

It is always lovely to hear from our consumers particularly when the comments are so complimentary.

I have enclosed a colour brochure showing the history of Branston Pickle since its launch in 1922, which I thought you might be interested in. Of course there have, more recently, been quite dramatic events in the life of Branston, with the fire last November at the pickle factory in Bury St Edmunds, where Branston is produced. As you are probably aware, this resulted in a great deal of media attention, due to a perceived shortage of Britain's best loved pickle around Christmas time. I am, however, please to report that the factory is now up and running to full capacity and Branston is thriving!

I do hope that you will always continue to enjoy Branston and have attached a voucher, which I hope you will accept with our compliments towards your next purchase, perhaps, if you haven't already, you might like to try our new relishes.

Thank you once again for contacting us and for your kind words.

Yours sincerely

Brontë Stump
Consumer Relations Administrator

Enc. voucher £ 1.00

Premier Foods, Bridge Road, Long Sutton, Spalding, Lincs PE12 9EQ Telephone: 01406 367000 Facsimile: 01406 364948
Consumer Services: Freephone 0800 032 0375. Lines are open Monday to Friday. 9.30am to 5pm
Premier Ambient Products (UK) Ltd, Registered in England, number 4427006, Registered Office: 28 The Green, Kings Norton, Birmingham B38 8SD

Mark Hebblewhite
Belmont Hill
Douglas
Isle of Man

Bronte Stump
Consumer Relations Advisor
Crosse and Blackwell
Premier Foods
Bridge Road
Long Sutton
Spalding
Lincs
PE12 9EQ

12th September 2005

Dear Bronte

Thank you for your letter dated 7th September. Firstly can I apologise for not being able to spell your name correctly due to the fact that my typewriter does not have the e with dots facility. Can I assume you are Scandinavian in origin? Thank you so much for the informative brochure detailing the history of your pickle. I have read it to my work colleagues and they were spellbound and hung upon my every word. I am sorry to have been misinformed that Sir Richard Branston is not associated with your product although on reflection this is perhaps a good thing as I am not keen on whiskers in my pickle.

I am very sorry to hear about the fire last Christmas but I would like to report that I have stocked up this year in case there is another shortfall. With further reference to your unfortunate fire look on the bright side, I like my pickle hot on occasion. Perhaps there is some fire damaged stock that I am able to purchase on the cheap? Thank you also for the information on famous admirers of your pickle products including Keith Richards; I have never thought of snorting your product but I am willing to try anything once. Please could you advise me if there is any way I can purchase your pickle in bulk (20 litres or more) so I can have a tank outside thus rendering numerous visits to the shops unnecessary. I would be grateful for your assistance with this matter.

Yours faithfully

Mark Hebblewhite.

Mark Hebblewhite

Mark Hebblewhite
Belmont Hill
Douglas
Isle of Man

Joy Williams
Federation of British Bonsai Societies
17 Woodland Park
Ynystawe
Swansea
SA6 5AR

29th August 2005

Dear Joy

I am writing to tell you about the problems I have experienced with my bonsai and also to inform you of the radical new approach to keeping trees that I have adopted. I bought my wife a bonsai from Marks and Spencer's for Christmas last year but unfortunately it only lasted until April before its condition had deteriorated to the extent that I had to dispose of it. We followed all the instructions in caring for it (the tree) so I can only assume it was not properly cared for at the shop. As a result my wife no longer considers herself green-fingered. We have got round this problem by 'adopting a tree' as it were. I have found that by looking at a normal size tree (but from further away) I can derive the same pleasure that my bonsai gave to me with none of the drawbacks. My 'bonsai' is located on the A59 Preston to Liverpool road just past the roundabout on the approach to the village of Garstang. Should you ever be passing I would love to hear your comments on it. I look forward to your comments on how my solution may increase the popularity of our hobby.

Yours faithfully

Mark Hebblewhite.

Mark Hebblewhite

Federation of British Bonsai Societies

Please reply to:-
General Secretary
Mrs. J.Williams
17 Woodland Park
Ynystawe
Swansea
SA6 5AR

Tel:-01792 845859
Fax:-
eMail:- secretary@fobbsbonsai.co.uk

Your Ref:-

Our Ref:-

Date:- 5th September 2005

Dear Mr.Hebblewhite,

Thank you for your letter. You and so many people before you have purchased these little trees and a large percentage of them have died. This is nothing to do with your husbandry of the tree but rather the long time it takes from their growing fields in the Far East to your doorstep. They are transported on container ships to Holland and spend a considerable time in loading bays so it is not surprising that their life is shortened. However, please do not give up on your quest for a bonsai. You can do this yourself. Firstly get yourself a good book from W.H.Smith or any good book shop. If no shops near you then www.amazon.co.uk There you will find excellent books at a low cost. I recommend the complete book of bonsai by Harry Tomlinson, the first book I bought, or one by Craig Coussins. These show you how it is done stage by stage. Secondly, get yourself down to a garden centre and buy a small pine or larch or conifer or beech tree or any small tree and do it yourself. You will need bonsai wire which some garden centres sell or get on-line.Bonsai wire is unlike any other as it is very pliable. There is no need to buy various sizes as you can use a few strands together. Sufficient when starting out.
There is no need to buy a bonsai as such. Another bit of information is that most enthusiasts keep their trees outdoors, this does not apply to semi-tropical species. You can bonsai anything! All it takes is patience. You may have in your garden a tree or shrub which you're tired of then dig it up put into a large ordinary pot or bucket and slowly work on that. Hope that this information helps you.

As for looking at nature, this is from where most bonsaists get their inspiration.
As for tools there are only three tools which are necessary. Branch cutters, concave cutters and wire cutters. Any sharp scissors will suffice. Christmas is coming and all these may be bought via mail order.

Good luck but be warned this could become an obsession

Yours truly,

Mrs. J.Williams

For on behalf of :-
Federation of British Bonsai Societies

Page 1 of 2

Friends of the National Bonsai Collection

Registered Office
3 Moor End, Eaton Bray, Dunstable,
Bedfordshire, LU6 2HN
Registered Number
2472361
A Company Limited by Guarantee

Mark Hebblewhite
Belmont Hill
Douglas
Isle of Man

General Secretary
Mrs J. Williams
Federation of British Bonsai Societies
17 Woodland Park
Ynystawe
Swansea
SA6 5AR

8th September 2005

Dear Joy

Have you seen my tree yet?

Yours faithfully

Mark Hebblewhite.

Mark Hebblewhite

Mark Hebblewhite
Belmont Hill
Douglas
Isle of Man

Kathy
Property Repair Systems
Salisbury House
Salisbury Road
Newton Abbot
Devon
TQ12 2DF

6th September 2005

Dear Kathy

On 14th October I intend to mount a protest against cheap adhesives by smearing myself with No Nails and adhering my body to the fascia of the headquarters of a substandard manufacturer of your choosing approximately 2ft from the ground. I shall, of course, be wearing a catsuit and swimming goggles for health and safety reasons. I would be grateful if you could provide me with a list of all those manufacturers of inferior products and highlight your most despised in red ink. Whilst I am sure that you will greatly appreciate this selfless act in defence of your industry I ask no thanks in return, merely a character reference in order to assist in my forthcoming interview at B and Q where it is my sincere wish that I am offered secure employment in charge of adhesives, sealants and, dependant on my performance at interview, masking tape and lubricants.

I look forward to your response.

Yours sincerely

Mark Hebblewhite.

Mark Hebblewhite

Property Repair Systems
Manufacturers of the Patented Timber Resin Splice

Unit 2
Salisbury House
Salisbury Road
Newton Abbot
Devon
TQ12 2DF

Tel: 01626 331351
Fax: 01626 331143
e-mail: dcmoore@timber.org.uk
Web: http://www.timber-repair.co.uk

Mark Hebblewhite

Douglas
Isle Of Man

September 8, 2005

Dear Mark,

Re: Adhesives Protest - your letter dated 6th September

We are pleased to support your protest against the cheap importation of adhesives from Sark - it is an outrage that British offshore islands are allowed to undercut the heavily taxed mainland manufacturers in this way and we applaud your plucky British Tommy, stiff upper lip, good loser aplomb, guts and general Englishness.

Your catsuit figure hugging body stocking is an inspired idea, but we recommend a more permanent adhesive, perhaps our Thixotropic Epoxy Body Stocking Self-smearing Megatrope, available at all good Transvestite Stores. This will withstand the British winter and the more taxing UV derived from Global Warming, as you will no doubt wish to pursue your protest over several seasons until your demise (we sense a deep commitment in your text, which was truly heartwarming for our Staff to read - many were moved to tears).

We have no hesitation in recommending you to B&Q - correctly bonded, we are sure that you have a secure future on the facia of your nearest B&Q branch and that you will increase their sales of adhesives - although we are not so sure that you have demonstrated any particular flair for lubricants (perhaps you would care to elaborate?).

Good luck and best wishes - don't forget to wave our Placard at the Media - please find attached our list of demands etched on waterproof lycra, which has been carefully chosen by our fashion department (Dave, in Packing) to match your ensemble.

Yours sincerely,

Kathy Moore (Mrs.)
Glupemeistress

Property Repair Systems VAT Registration No. 443 5188 47
National Epoxy Resins Distributors

Mark Hebblewhite (Mr)
Belmont Hill
Douglas
Isle of Man

Kathy Moore (Mrs)
Property Repair Systems
Unit 2
Salisbury House
Salisbury Road
Newton Abbot
Devon
TQ12 2DF

13th September 2005

Dear Kathy

I am most heartened that you have decided to support my adhesive protest on the 14th October (weather permitting). Thank you also for your words of encouragement – I applaud your applauding of my plucky British Tommy. I am pleased to announce I have indeed been successful in my B and Q interview where I am soon to be responsible for adhesives, sealants, masking tape, lubricants and, as an added bonus, I will be keeping an eye on abrasive products including sanding blocks but not discs as Eric looks after discs apparently.

With response to your query as to my experience with lubricants, I enclose a copy of my query and job application to the British Lubrication Federation, who are currently considering whether or not there is a role for me in the industry. I would be extremely grateful if you could pass on my thanks to Dave (in packing) for his contribution to my protest which was greatly appreciated. I imagine that with Dave's commitment the packing department is a model of efficiency. Remember, Dave, the packing department of an adhesive company is like the engine room of a large ship. Bravo and keep up the good work, Dave!

I have taken on board your comments about the use of a more permanent adhesive in my protest. However, it has proven difficult to locate a reliable supply of Thixotropic epoxy body stocking self-smearing megatrope – the staff at the local Wilkinson's have proved less than helpful so far. As an added bonus to yourself, Kathy, and the staff at Property Repair Systems, I have decided that my protest needs a dual purpose and to that end I will be attempting to raise public awareness of the patented Timber Resin Splice by making one and wearing it as a hat. I am assuming they look similar to Tunnock's Caramel Logs; please advise.

Best wishes

Mark Hebblewhite.

Mark Hebblewhite

Mark Hebblewhite
Belmont Hill
Douglas
Isle of Man

Peter Ashwell
Bedford Astronomical Society
12 Irthing Close
Brickhill
Bedford
MK41 7TP

6th September 2005

Dear Peter

I am writing to you because I have a question which you may be able to answer for me. If I could travel faster than the speed of light from my house to the discount tyre centre I can see out of the window, when I got there would I be able to see my own image coming towards me (in the same way that light from long dead stars is still visible on earth)? Also I have heard that anything that could travel at the speed of light would shrink by a third in size. If this is the case, since I am 6ft 8 tall would I be able to pass through my bathroom door (if I ran towards it at the speed of light) without banging my head? Many thanks in anticipation of your help with these dilemmas which have been troubling me for a while.

Yours faithfully

Mark Hebblewhite.

Mark Hebblewhite

Bedford Astronomical Society

Publications Editor and Membership Secretary
Peter Ashwell, 12 Irthing Close, Brickhill, Bedford MK41 7TP
T: 01234 211532 F: 01234 353777 E: newsletter@bedsastro.org.uk

www.bedsastro.org.uk

Founded January 1987

Mark Hebblewhite

Douglas
Isle of Man

13th September 2005

Dear Mark,

Thank you for your recent letter concerning the speed of light and your height. Even though, in your hypothesis, you are travelling at the speed of light or greater, your entity can only be in one place in time and space as 'seen' by another viewer. For instance, stars that are light years distant from our view point on Earth that have already evolved and died are still seen by us at their earlier stages of development. Also, for things travelling faster than light such as in a black hole where you cannot see matter at all you would therefore not be able to see your own image coming towards you.

Matter cannot stay in its original chemical or molecular form at the speed of light and would completely change at a greater speed. Also in a black hole you would not be able to see anything anyway.

In theory you would be 'stretched' in time and space and therefore taller and not shorter. That would mean you could bang your head on the top of your door opening or potentially not be able to go through it at all due to your now vast size. However in this state your head and feet would be in a different time and space, as would the door so there would still be the possibility of getting a bump on the head due to your relative sizes. But in this state you would be suffering many other adverse effects anyway so your concussion would be 'immaterial'.

In conclusion I think we could both get headaches without leaving the room through just thinking about this conundrum so lets not go into this any further please.

Regards,

Peter Ashwell

Mark Hebblewhite
Belmont Hill
Douglas
Isle of Man

The Hill Brush Company
Woodlands Road
Mere
Wiltshire
BA12 6BS

6th September 2005

Dear Sir or Madam

I am writing to advise you of an organisation which has recently been set up to promote and market the British brush making industry and to invite you to register your company's details for inclusion on our national retailers database and website, sweeper. co.uk, due to go 'live' mid October 2005.

Market research conducted with the help of a leading UK hardware chain has established that 'brushing' as opposed to the use of vacuum cleaners is enjoying something of a comeback with the growing popularity of laminate flooring as opposed to traditional floor coverings due to reasons of economy (for obvious reasons) and to some extent exercise, in that regular sweeping provides an excellent cardiovascular workout.

To give you a little history in the origins of the company and my experience in the brush making industry, I have been making brushes for nearly 15 years under the brand name 'Sweeper', which stands for:

SWEEP
WHEN
EXTRA
EFFORT
PRODUCES
EXTRAORDINARY
RESULTS

My interest in brushes (and to some extent career) began in 1990 as I watched my father attempt to clean a concrete pathway with a brush that was both ill designed and ineffective. Even at the age of 19 I realised that futile attempts at cleaning with an inferior product were slowly and surely leading to the demise of a craft and an industry that have been around for longer than many people think. Shortly afterwards in 1992 I began the small scale production of 'soft brushes' comprised of a 90/10 viscose/cat hair mix for use on wooden flooring. Although production quantities were low initially due to reliance on one feline's output of 200 grams PA, I was able to slowly build the business over a period of 10 years to a turnover approaching 12K and growing!

I would welcome a response from your company as to your inclusion on our database and website (which is of course free). All I would ask is that you would give some consideration to the marketing of my unique product in your stores.

I look forward to your response.

Mark Hebblewhite.

Mark Hebblewhite

BY APPOINTMENT TO H.M. THE QUEEN
MANUFACTURERS OF BRUSHWARE

THE HILL BRUSH COMPANY LTD

WOODLANDS ROAD   MERE   WILTSHIRE BA12 6BS   ENGLAND
Telephone: 01747 860494   Fax: 01747 860137   e-mail: info@hillbrush.com   website: www.hillbrush.com
Sales Telephone: 01747 861766   Sales Fax: 01747 861767   e-mail: sales@hillbrush.com

20 September 2005

PWC/le

Mark Hebblewhite

Douglas
Isle of Man

Dear Mr Hebblewhite

With reference to your letter dated 6th September 2005, we were interested to read about
your proposed website sweeper.co.uk, which you say will go live in mid October. To be
honest before we become involved in any websites we like to see the finishes article so I
would be grateful if you could contact me when the site is live.

Regards

Yours sincerely
pp THE HILL BRUSH COMPANY LTD

Philip W Coward
Managing Director

Mark Hebblewhite
Belmont Hill
Douglas
Isle of Man

Philip Coward
The Hill Brush Company Ltd
Woodlands Road
Mere
Wiltshire
BA12 6BS

24th September 2005

Dear Philip

Many thanks for your letter dated 20th September. I understand your reluctance as an established company to become involved with my website until you have had the chance to review it. I regret to inform you that I have had to put back the launch date due to lack of demand from brush manufacturers. Would it be possible to send you some more information/pictures on/of my products in use on laminate flooring in order to get your opinion on them? I would also be interested in learning a little more about how you have built up your business to its current level of success.

Yours faithfully

Mark Hebblewhite.

Mark Hebblewhite

BY APPOINTMENT TO H.M. THE QUEEN
MANUFACTURERS OF BRUSHWARE

THE HILL BRUSH COMPANY LTD

WOODLANDS ROAD   MERE   WILTSHIRE BA12 6BS   ENGLAND

Telephone: 01747 860494   Fax: 01747 860137   e-mail: info@hillbrush.com   website: www.hillbrush.com

Sales Telephone: 01747 861766   Sales Fax: 01747 861767   e-mail: sales@hillbrush.com

05 October 2005

PWC/le

Mark Hebblewhite

Douglas
Isle of Man

Dear Mr Hebblewhite

With reference to your letter dated 24th September 2005, we are sorry to hear that you have had to put back the launch date of your website.

We would be interested to receive more information and pictures of your products for use on laminate flooring.

With regard to our own business, our company was started in 1922 by my Grandfather and his brother, and as you can see from the enclosed history, written by my father, the company has expanded since its formation. We now have our main plant in the UK and a small plant in Baltimore USA manufacturing horse grooming brushes.

Most of the information regarding the history of the company is in the enclosed brochure.

Regards

Yours sincerely
pp THE HILL BRUSH COMPANY LTD

Philip W Coward
Managing Director

DIRECTORS
P W COWARD B.Tech
M D COWARD
P R COWARD (USA)

REGISTERED OFFICE MERE WILTSHIRE
REGISTERED IN ENGLAND No. 3464746
VAT REG No GB 188 0464 40

Mark Hebblewhite
Belmont Hill
Douglas
Isle of Man

Philip Coward
The Hill Brush Company Ltd
Woodlands Road
Mere
Wiltshire
BA12 6BS

10th October 2005

Dear Philip

Thank you for your letter dated 5th October. My demonstration type photos of my latest sweeping product in use on a laminate floor are being developed at the moment and I will send them shortly. I am afraid it looks as though I am going to have to scrap my plans for a website due to a poor response but I would like to thank both yourself and the Hill Brush Company for the interest and enthusiasm you have shown in both my idea and products.

Thank you also for the informative literature you kindly sent. I was amazed to find out that your company manufactures horse grooming brushes in Baltimore. I have read with great interest the history of the company you sent me. I have noticed that on page 11 where Len Hardcastle is examining the gumati fibre from Indonesia it looks as though he has something in his pocket. Was he ever accused of pilfering, as I would hate to think he was selling brush heads or gumati fibre to line his pocket at your expense?

I look forward to your response.

Yours faithfully

Mark Hebblewhite.

Mark Hebblewhite

Mark Hebblewhite
Belmont Hill
Douglas
Isle of Man

Les Preston
Welsh Black Cattle Society of England
Coombe Farm
Green Hitchings
Great Milton
Oxfordshire
OX44 7NZ

12th September 2005

Dear Mr Preston

I too am black, Welsh and proud. I was born in 1972 in Swansea and moved over to the Isle of Man in 2001 to assist with the running of my late grandfather's farm. We currently have 50 in the herd which I am most proud of. I was delighted to hear about your organisation through a friend as, although I was born in Wales and proud to be Welsh, I am first and foremost a black farmer and we are few and far between in the United Kingdom. It really is good to know that I am not alone. Please could you forward details of how I may join your organisation together with any programme of social events that you have planned. I am very excited to have found your organisation and cannot wait to meet the other members. In particular, I am looking for a wife, although I am not fussy about where she comes from. Many thanks for your assistance with these matters and I wish you and your organisation all the best.

Yours faithfully

Mark Hebblewhite.

Mark Hebblewhite

WELSH BLACK BREEDERS ASSOCIATION
OF ENGLAND
EST. 1975
(Members of Welsh Black Cattle Society)

Hon. Sec/Fieldsman
Les Preston
01844 279718
07767 870169

Coombe Farm
Green Hitchings
Great Milton
Oxfordshire
OX44 7NZ

5·10·05

DEAR MARU

SORRY FOR BEING SO SLOW IN REPLYING TO YOUR LETTER MANY THANKS FOR THAT, I HAVE BEEN RATHER BUSY ORGANIZING OUR AGM WHICH WE ARE HOLDING THIS WEEKEND THE 9th OF OCT. IN BRIANKSPUDDLE IN DORSET.

DID YOU SAY YOU HAVE WELSH BLACK CATTLE WHAT IS YOUR PREFIX OF THE HERD?

I WILL SEND YOU OUR JOURNAL FOR THE YEAR WHEN I GET A NEW SUPPLY, WE DO NOT HAVE A GREAT SOCIAL EVENTS CALENDER BUT I DO SEND OUT NEWSLETTERS ABOUT TWICE A YEAR, WOULD YOU PLEASE RING AT SOMETIME AS YOU DID NOT INCLUDE YOUR TELEPHONE NUMBER

BEST WISHES

Les Preston

SEC/FIELDSMAN
W.B.B.A.E

Council Representatives

Yvonne Brown
Gloucestershire
01608 674363

Les Preston
Oxfordshire
01844 279718

John Dimery-Seek
Somerset
01749 672344

WELSH BLACK BREEDERS ASSOCIATION
OF ENGLAND
EST. 1975
(Members of Welsh Black Cattle Society)

Hon. Sec/Fieldsman
Les Preston
01844 279718
07767 870169

Coombe Farm
Green Hitchings
Great Milton
Oxfordshire
OX44 7NZ

AGENDA & NOTICE OF THE 26TH AGM OF THE ABOVE ASSOCIATION
ON SUNDAY 9TH OCTOBER 2005 AT BLACKDOWN HOUSE BRIANTSPUDDLE,
DORSET 12NOON SHARP.

 ✱ FOR VENUE PLEASE SEE NOTE BELOW. ✱

1. Apologies

2. Minutes of 2004 AGM

3. Matters Arising

4. Support AOB Bath & West Show for 2006 ?

5. Sec/Fieldsman report for 2005 including income & expenditure.

6. Andrew James Chief Executive to address meeting.

7. Enzo Sauro to address members.

8. Any other business.

9. Date and Venue of 2006 AGM October 8th by kind permission of Pertwood
Partners, Hindon, Wiltshire, home of the Warden Herd of polled organic
Welsh Blacks.

MEMBERS PLEASE NOTE :- GO STRAIGHT TO BRIANTSPUDDLE VILLAGE HALL FOR
MEETING & BUFFET. ROAD NO'S TO BRIANTSPUDDLE A35 THEN B3390. ALL ROUTES
WILL BE SIGNED WITH THE BLACK BULL SIGNS INCLUDING TO *THE VILLAGE HALL*

BUFFET BOOKING SLIP

I would like to book buffet lunch for (   ) persons.

Please return slip by 1st October or phone 01844-279718.

(There is no charge)

Les Preston

Les Preston
Hon/Sec/Fieldsman
W.B.B.A.E.

Council Representatives

Yvonne Brown	Les Preston	Roger Winsor
Gloucestershire	Oxfordshire	Devon

130

Mark Hebblewhite
Belmont Hill
Douglas
Isle of Man

Professor Steve Elliot
Institute of Sound and Vibration Research
University Road
Highfield
Southampton
S017 1BJ

20th September 2005

Dear Steve

My wife and I would very much like to join the research group but I am not sure if we are eligible as we do not live in the Southampton area and my wife does not possess any recognised scientific qualifications and I only got a D in physics. We have been carrying out experiments at home in our improvised laboratory (also our bathroom) for over 2 years concerned with measuring the ability and distance travelled underwater of different frequencies at different temperatures. Our findings so far as follows. Provided the meniscus (surface) is undisturbed and the water is tepid, I am able to shout at my wife underwater from one end of the bath and she can clearly understand every word I say. Providing we can hold our breath long enough, she is able to reply using a high pitched squeal which is clearly audible at my end (although she sometimes emits this noise in response to her proximity to the hot taps as opposed to my initial underwater outburst). We have found that higher frequencies travel best, especially when we do not use bubble bath, although we are still unsure of the reason for this. We would be grateful if you could advise us if you are able to use the results of our experiments, which I would be delighted to send. Also, could you advise me why bubble bath affects our experiment's success to such a degree.

I look forward to your reply.

Yours faithfully

Mark Hebblewhite.

Mark Hebblewhite

University of Southampton

Institute of Sound and Vibration Research

Fluid Dynamics and Acoustics Group

University of Southampton
Highfield
Southampton
SO17 1BJ
United Kingdom

Telephone +44 (0)23 8059 2291
Fax +44 (0)23 8059 3190

27 September 2005

Mr Mark Hebblethwaite

Douglas
Isle of Man

Dear Mr Hebblethwaite

Professor Steve Elliott has asked me to respond to the letter which you wrote to him on 20 September 2005. Underwater measurements in reverberant environments such as baths (I assume your bath is the usual domestic size) are notoriously difficult. With a sound speed underwater of around 1500 m/s then it will take sound only about 1/1000th of a second to travel from one end of the bath the other in the water in the water. However this transmission will be complicated by reflections from the walls which I estimate will start complicating the signal about 1/10,000th of a second after its inception. Furthermore, signals will enter the wall of the bath and propagate through there, re-radiating sound back into the water. Hence it is extremely difficult to make clear observations that are unadulterated by reflections. I do not feel what I will be able to make competent use of any data that you have taken.

The issue of bubble bath is an interesting one. In principle, the addition of surfactants to the water will stabilise the population small bubbles (I refer here to the underwater bubbles, which are spheres of gas surrounded by water, as opposed to the surface foam bubbles which are gas pocket surrounded by thin layers of liquid, outside of which is more gas). The presence of bubbles will in principle absorb more sound. However it is impossible for me to suggest whether the effect would properly the observable without knowledge of the bubble population and the acoustic signals you propagate.

I should warn that the manner in which of conducting these experiments is not best suited to scientific investigation. Verbal methods of sound production can lack the reproducibility required to test theories properly. Subjective measurement methods, exploiting hearing, are notoriously difficult to interpret, since not only can the signal your monitoring change, but the subjective measurement can suffer perturbations: therefore if you detect a change, you not know whether the observable itself is changing or whether the monitoring system is changing.

In summary I regret to inform you that I do not feel your approach would tally well with the mathematically-based, objective, and quantitative approach which I insist is adopted by those who work in my own laboratory. I am pleased that you are enjoying your investigations, but I regret I am not able to provide a platform or environment which could either host your investigations or analyse your findings.

Yours faithfully,

Professor Tim Leighton
Professor of Ultrasonics and Underwater Acoustics
Institute of Sound Vibration Research

Mark Hebblewhite
Belmont Hill
Douglas
Isle of Man

Professor Tim Leighton
Professor of Ultrasonics and Underwater Acoustics
University Road
Highfield
Southampton
S017 1BJ

10th October 2005

Dear Dr Tim

Thank you for your letter dated 27th September. With regard to your queries about my underwater experiments, the bath in which we carry them out is indeed a domestic one. The acoustic signal propagated by my wife is generally 'Ayyieeeeeeeeeeeeeeeeeeeah' and the bubble population you refer to is provided courtesy of Tescos (49p for 1 litre of bathtime fun).

I am very sorry to learn that you are not able to use the results of my experiments as they do not have a quantitative approach. This being the case we have ceased our scientific investigations immediately on your advice and we have once more taken up heavy drinking, which is a shame as I felt we were on the verge of a breakthrough. On a positive note, if you feel we are able to contribute to your organisation at any level I would be very pleased to hear from you.

Yours faithfully

Mark Hebblewhite.

Mark Hebblewhite

Mark Hebblewhite
Belmont Hill
Douglas
Isle of Man

Greens Flours Ltd
Station Road
Maldon
Essex
CM9 4LQ

20th September 2005

Dear Sir or Madam

I am writing to request your advice on increasing the annual turnover of my company. I have been given your address by directory enquiries staff.

I have very recently left full time education and have just opened what I hope will be a successful venture in the flour retail industry. I am currently employing just one part time member of staff in order to keep down costs which means that any profit I make can be put back into the business. During the opening weak the store took £250 (approx £60 profit) which I feel was a good start, bearing in mind my product range was limited.

Over the next weak or so I hope to increase my product range to include wreaths and seasonal buckeuts in order to get more customers. I would be very grateful for any help you can offer me as I am finding it very difficult to get good business advice due to my age. Thank you for taking the time to reed my letter and I hope to hear from you soon.

Yours sincerely

Mark Hebblewhite.

Mark Hebblewhite

GREENS FLOUR MILLS LIMITED

Station Road, Maldon, Essex CM9 4LQ England
Telephone: 01621 852696 Fax: 01621 854525

Mr M Hebblewhite

Douglas
Isle of Man

21 September 2005

Dear Mr Hebblewhite

Thank you for your letter of 20th September 2005, however, I think that the directories staff has misled you.

We are not florist's and have nothing to do with this industry, we are actually millers and produce flour for baking.

I am sorry we are not in a position to help, and hope that you get answers to your questions.

Yours sincerely

Pat Rhodes
Administrator

Registered in England No. 3446763 - Registered Office: Station Road, Maldon

Mark Hebblewhite
Belmont Hill
Douglas
Isle of Man

Pat Rhodes
Greens Flours Ltd
Station Road
Maldon
Essex
CM9 4LQ

24th September 2005

Dear Pat

Thank you very much for your letter. I am very sorry for the confusin I may have caused due to my poor spelling. I have had the signe above the shop changed to 'Marks Flowers' instead of 'Marks Flours' and bussiness picked up immidiatelly and the customers do not laugh no more. Many thanks for your best wishes and although you are in the flour and not the flower industry if you have any good tips for me they would be appraciatted a lot.

Yours faithfully

Mark Hebblewhite.

Mark Hebblewhite

Mark Hebblewhite
Belmont Hill
Douglas
Isle of Man

The Right Honourable Alistair Darling MP
Great Minster House
76 Marsham Street
London
SW1P 4DR

20th September 2005

Dear Mr Darling

I would like to invite you to attend an event I am organising on 15th October at the Claremont Hotel in Douglas. If you have ever visited the island I am sure that you are aware that the Isle of Man lacks a modern system of public transport and it is this that I intend to address at our meeting on 15th.

I have already raised enough funds over the last 7 years to construct the first leg of what will be the Douglas to Ballakermeen Steam Railway and with your support and knowledge of transport infrastructures I am sure you could stimulate what is certain to be a lively debate. It is hoped that the construction of the track will be the first step in ensuring that commuters from the outlying areas of Douglas will no longer have to suffer the agonising commute to the central area of the town. I do hope you are able to support me in this cause and I look forward to your response.

Yours faithfully

Mark Hebblewhite.

Mark Hebblewhite

**From the Office of
the Secretary of State**

Mr Mark Hebblewhite

Douglas
Isle of Man

Department for
Transport

Great Minster House
76 Marsham Street
London SW1P 4DR

Tel: 020 7944 3011
Fax: 020 7944 4399
E-Mail: alistair.darling@dft.gsi.gov.uk

Web site: www.dft.gov.uk

6 OCTOBER 2005

Dear Mark Hebblewhite,

Thank you for your invitation to Alistair Darling MP, to attend an event in Douglas on 15th October 05.

I regret that the Secretary of State will be unable to attend on this occasion. However, may I take this opportunity to wish you every success with this event.

Regards,

**ANNABELLE HADLAND
ASSISTANT DIARY SECRETARY**

Mark Hebblewhite
Belmont Hill
Douglas
Isle of Man

Peter Ashcroft
Walking the Way to Health Initiative
The Countryside Agency
John Dower House
Crescent Place
Cheltenham
GL50 3RA

20th September 2005

Dear Peter

My wife and I have enjoyed walking for many years now and during this time it has occurred to us that unless the pastime grows in popularity with young people we may steadily see footpaths and rights of way ignored by landowners due to lack of demand. I am not a member of your organisation but nevertheless I hope you will not object if I put forward an idea that I feel may contribute to an increase in the popularity of walking in the younger generations.

My wife and I recently organised a 3-mile walk in aid of charity through a local glen with the support of a local youth group. The initial response was slow to say the least as walking is perceived as a pastime for 'oldies' such as myself and my wife. However we were able to encourage 60 youths to join us on an experience they may not otherwise have enjoyed by giving the walk what I believe is called a 'hip hop' theme. For the day I became 'Mr Boombastic', my role being to lead the way. My wife took up the rear to ensure there were no stragglers. We 'hot stepped' as opposed to walked for the majority of the journey and it was an experience enjoyed by all, and one that I hope to repeat soon.

I would be grateful if you could advise me whether or not your organisation has any plans in place to protect the future of our pastime with regard to enticing young people into the fold.

I would be extremely grateful for your comments, thoughts, and any advice you could give me for future activities.

Yours sincerely

Mark Hebblewhite.

Mr and Mrs Hebblewhite

Douglas
Isle of Man

The Countryside Agency

Landscape Access Recreation

Walking the Way to Health
John Dower House, Crescent Place
Cheltenham, Gloucestershire GL50 3RA

Telephone   01242 533 299
Switchboard 01242 521 381
Fax   01242 584 270

www.countryside.gov.uk

ENTICING YOUNG PEOPLE TO WALK

Dear Mark

Thanks very much for your letter about the relative lack of young people who enjoy walking. I was very impressed by the inventiveness of your 'hip hop' theme and it sounds like it was really successful in getting younger people along.

While the target audience of WHI tends to be sedentary people over 50, there are other initiatives within the Countryside Agency and beyond which try to encourage children to walk more. One such example I'm aware of is the Walking Bus scheme, where children walk to school in a group with two or more parent volunteers – a 'driver' who leads the way and a 'conductor' at the rear. The walking bus follows a set route with agreed pick up points. The catchment of the service can be extended in a rural area by establishing a 'park and ride' bus stop, where parents from outlying areas can wait with their children and allow them to continue their journey on foot. The 'Diversity Review' team here are researching how best to get young people active in the countryside and an approach they are piloting is getting an inner city group of children with an interest in cricket out into the countryside to play a team from a rural area.

You may find incentives helpful, for example, on of our walking groups in Wrexham have an agreement with the council whereby walkers rewarded with £5 vouchers for fruit and vegetables for every four walks they attended. The vouchers can be exchanged at one particular fruit and vegetable outlet in Wrexham.

I hope you continue to come up with successful initiatives and would be interested to hear of any ideas you have to encourage more young people to go walking. If you wanted to set up a

The Countryside Agency

**Landscape
Access
Recreation**

regular WHI group, maybe aimed at younger people, then we could send you a pack – tel 01242 533258.

Hope this helps.

Yours sincerely

Moira Halstead

Moira Halstead
WHI Marketing and Development Manager

Helping everyone to respect, protect and enjoy the countryside

Mark Hebblewhite
Belmont Hill
Douglas
Isle of Man

Moira Halstead
WHI Marketing and Development Manager
The Countryside Agency
Walking the Way to Health
John Dower House
Crescent Place
Cheltenham
Gloucestershire
GL50 3RA

25th October 2005

Dear Moira

Thank you for your letter dated 19th October. I am most pleased that you liked the idea of my 'hip hop' themed walks. We were impressed with the fruit and vegetable voucher scheme you mentioned in Wrexham and my wife and I have decided to try and implement a similar idea on the Isle of Man, substituting fruit and vegetables for cigarettes and/or crisps which we feel would have a broader appeal. My wife and I would be very interested in setting up a Walking the Way to Health group as you mentioned in your letter and we would be most grateful if you could arrange to forward a pack so we can get underway as soon as possible.

Kind regards

Mark Hebblewhite.

Mr and Mrs Hebblewhite

Mark Hebblewhite
Belmont Hill
Douglas
Isle of Man

Computime Systems Ltd
4 Woodside Mews
Clayton Wood Close
Leeds
LS16 6QE

20th September 2005

Dear Sir

I have recently invented a time management system that I feel may be of interest to your company. It is a voice activated clocking in machine which is capable of performing all the functions of traditional time management systems. For short I have called my device 'the voice activated clocking in machine'.

It works on a similar basis to the systems used by the Pentagon in many films you may have seen in which the President cannot launch a nuclear strike without his eyeballs being read by a laser, the marked difference being that 'the voice activated clocking in machine' is not dependent on lasers or eyeballs but merely on the human voice. Once set up and initialised by myself the machine would work as follows.

"It's Dean, I'm off for my dinner."

(Machine recognises Dean's voice and with the use of clever electrics knows that he has one hour.)

"It's Dean, I'm back from my dinner but I'm 4 minutes late cos I dropped my cheese and onion pasty on my trousers and had to go to the bus station toilets to clean them."

(Machine recognises Dean is a workshy hound and automatically deducts 15 minutes' pay from his salary for lying.)

The 'voice activated clocking in machine' can also be used to resolve disputes about who had the earliest dinner last week, for example.

"Who had the earliest dinner last week?"

(Machine replies, "It was Margaret; her mother was poorly.")

Please feel free to contact me should you require any further information about my machine. A prompt reply would be appreciated as I expect demand to 'go through the roof' once word gets about.

Yours sincerely

Mark Hebblewhite.

Mark Hebblewhite

computime®
systems

Mr Mark Hebblewhite

Douglas
Isle of Man

21st September 2005

Dear Mark

Thank you for your letter dated 20th September. As a Time and Attendance Supplier we are always interested in new and innovative products to market in the UK and abroad. Would you be kind enough to send me further information on your voice activated time management Terminal.

Yours sincerely

Ben Lassoued
Managing Director

Computime Systems UK Ltd   Tel: +44 (0) 113 2302002   Company Registration No: 3221489
4 Woodside Mews   Fax: +44 (0) 113 2200330   VAT No: 647691203
Clayton Wood Close
Leeds   Email: sales@computimeuk.com
LS16 6QE   www.computimeuk.com

Mark Hebblewhite
Belmont Hill
Douglas
Isle of Man

Mr Ben Lassoued
Computime Systems Ltd
4 Woodside Mews
Clayton Wood Close
Leeds
LS16 6QE

24th September 2005

Dear Ben

Hooray and thank you for your letter!

As you requested I am writing to provide you with further information on the voice activated clocking in machine I have developed. (The voice activated clocking in machine for short.)

The device is currently in the process of being registered at the patent office and until this process is complete I am continuing to experiment with my device at home in that I am monitoring my wife's movements day to day. There are also a number of problems with the device to be ironed out before it can be put on the mass market (priced competitively at £299).

Firstly the machine becomes confused when used by anybody with a Bradford accent, which I am sure you understand. Secondly, although the machine can be used by any number of employees, it is not too good when employees have the same/similar names. This being the case it could not as yet be used by organisations employing members of the same family. I personally consider this to be a bonus because in my experience family members working for the same company (particularly if they are brothers and big) can prove to be an unruly and disruptive influence. They are also prone to stealing.

I would be happy to visit your premises at a time suitable to yourself in order to perform a demonstration should you desire it.

I look forward to your response.

Yours faithfully

Mark Hebblewhite.

Mark Hebblewhite

Ref: BL/JL

Mr Mark Hebblewhite

Douglas
Isle of Man

29th September 2005

Dear Mark

Good to hear from you. Could you please contact me to arrange a demonstration of your voice activated device.
My email address is ben@computimeuk.com

Kind Regards

Ben Lassoued

Managing Director

Computime Systems UK Ltd
4 Woodside Mews
Clayton Wood Close
Leeds
LS16 6QE

Tel: +44 (0) 113 2302002
Fax: +44 (0) 113 2200330

Email: sales@computimeuk.com
www.computimeuk.com

Company Registration No: 3721489
VAT No: 647691203

From: Mark Hebblewhite
To: Ben Lassoued
Subject: My Amazing Invention
Date: Mon 3rd Oct 2005

Dear Ben

I am most excited to have received your letter. I read it on the way to work and I was very nearly late in my excitement. I am encouraged by your enthusiasm to see my machine perform a demonstration. You will be most impressed, I can assure you. I am going on holiday for a week on 17th October and I'm afraid I can't be in Leeds before then as the people of Douglas would miss me too much, but if you would like me to visit your premises after the 24th October I would be most grateful. I can't make it on Tuesdays, however, as I am playing darts then. I am looking forward to us becoming very rich indeed. How many do you think we can sell?

(I am quite happy to see a 60/40 split in your favour.)

In my opinion we need to flog at least 10 as I have promised my wife she can have anything she wants from the Argos catalogue and also I have to buy enough creosote to sort the fence out before winter is upon us.

Kind regards

Mark Hebblewhite

----- Original Message Follows -----
From: Ben Lassoued
To: Mark Hebblewhite
Subject: RE: My Amazing Invention
Date: Wed 5th Oct 2005 13:37:37 +0100

Dear Mark

Nice to hear from you.

May I suggest 27th October for a meeting in Leeds.

Kind Regards

Ben Lassoued

From: Mark Hebblewhite
To: Ben Lassoued
Subject: My Amazing Invention
Date: Wed 5th October 2005

Ben

The 27th will be just fine. I hope you are as excited as I am. What time would you like me to attend? After 10am would suit me (Thursday 27th) if possible, due to flight times from the Isle of Man and also I need to find my battery charger (nickel cadmium) in order to ensure the VACIM operates to its normal level of efficiency. Please can you advise me if your premises has a staff canteen as I would very much like to have a cup of coffee prior to the demonstration as I find it quite nerve-racking. I currently opt for option 91, white, extra sugar and a bit frothy if that is possible.

Would you like me to bring anything over with me? At work we currently have a selection of fine toffee (made locally) or perhaps you would like a cat – I have 3 spare at this time. Alternatively I can consider bringing you a present from my holidays in the Canaries, perhaps a scale model of a small church designed by Caesar Manrique, a local hero apparently. Please advise.

Have you got any interested parties yet, Ben, as regards the VACIM?

Regards

Mark

Mark Hebblewhite
Belmont Hill
Douglas
Isle of Man

First Tunnels Ltd
Dixon Street
Barrowford
Lancashire
BB9 8PL

10th October 2005

Dear Sir or Madam

I am writing to ask for your assistance in an engineering project I am currently working on. I have a very attractive next-door neighbour with whom I am currently having a fling. So as to not arouse my wife's suspicions I am constructing a tunnel from the cupboard under my stairs to my next-door neighbour's pantry. We hope to meet up 2 metres south of my boiler cupboard providing my calculations are correct. The problem is that I have hit a bed of clay at the depth of 1 metre which I estimate to be 1.5 metres deep. I have established that the clay strata is at least this depth by poking it with a clothes pole. I would be extremely grateful if you could give me benefit of your experience by telling me firstly the best and quickest way to tunnel through hard clay. Secondly, are wooden props for the tunnel's ceiling sufficient to take the weight of clay over a distance of 11 metres as, although I find this lady very attractive, I have no wish to rush the job and risk suffocating due to a collapse. Please mark your reply STRICTLY PRIVATE AND CONFIDENTIAL.

Yours sincerely

Mark Hebblewhite.

Mark Hebblewhite

First Tunnels
The Number One Specialists in Polytunnels & Horticultural Supplies.

First Tunnels Limited
Dixon Street
Barrowford
Lancashire
BB9 8PL

Tel: 01282 601253
Fax: 01282 612420
Email: sales@firsttunnels.co.uk
Web: firsttunnels.co.uk

21/10/2005

Dear Mr Hebblewhite,

Let us congratulate you on your ingenuity.

We are not sure any woman however attractive is worth such an effort, and unfortunately you have confused our name with a company, which employs trolls working underground, whereas we are suppliers of plastic greenhouses called polytunnels. However we are always ready to help and the design team have put their heads together and come up with the following.

As you will be aware the channel tunnel is now complete and has been for some time, the tunnel boring machines used in this project are now mothballed and despite efforts to sell them no bidder has been found. We are in possession of information through a customer who runs a garden center in Dover and who's daughters boyfriends mates uncle lives secretly in the euro tunnel whilst awaiting his opportunity to enter France and claim refugee status. He states that any one of these machines can be purchased at a knock down price (estimated at £1) and driven under its own power under the south of England (avoiding Stonehenge) on under the Bristol channel, under the Irish sea to the I.O.M. By remaining under ground the machine could surface under your stairs without your wife's knowledge. As these machines lay a cylinder of concrete behind them as they move forward the problem you have come across regarding deep clay will be overcome. When complete a swing bridge could be suspended from the tunnel roof to give your neighbour the romantic image of her Tarzan entering from the pantry.

As with all plans there will be down sides. We estimate that the above project will take 8 years and wonder if your neighbour will still be as attractive on your return. The up side is you will emerge in a pantry and you may well be suffering from the onset of malnutrition after such a long period.

We admire your endeavors and wish you the best of luck.

Kind Regards

The First Tunnels Team

We supply...

❖ Polytunnels & Accessories   ❖ Cloches   ❖ Cold Frames
❖ Irrigation Systems   ❖ Garden Buildings   ❖ Greenhouse Heating
❖ Ground Covers   ❖ Nets & Fleece   ❖ Garden Lighting   ❖ Garden Tools
❖ Power Tools   ❖ Pots & Trays   ❖ Containers

Registered Office: 16-18 Devonshire Street, Keighley, West Yorkshire BD21 2DG
Company Reg No: 4196731 (Cardiff)

Mark Hebblewhite
Belmont Hill
Douglas
Isle of Man

BJ Sherriff Beekeeping Supplies
Carclew Road
Mylor Downs
Falmouth
Cornwall
TR11 5UN

10th October 2005

Dear Mr Sheriff

I have been given your details by the British Glove Association who thought you might be interested in my new and unique design for beekeeping gloves. As you can see, Mr Sherriff, they are unique in 2 ways. Firstly they allow the beekeeper to get as close to the hive as he wants with no risk of getting stung at all. Secondly, these gloves do not come as a pair, that's right, they do not come as a pair. I would not tell the customers this so we would make double the money if we sell by mail order. Please find enclosed my design and I look forward to your comments as to whether we are able to form a mutually beneficial business arrangement. I have a prototype available if you would like to see it.

I look forward to your comments.

Yours faithfully

Mark Hebblewhite.

Mark Hebblewhite

B J SHERRIFF INTERNATIONAL

Carclew Rd.Mylor Downs.Falmouth
Cornwall.TR11 5UN. England
Email: enquiries@bjsherriff.com

Tel + 44 (0) 1872 863304   Fax + 44 (0) 1872 865267

11. October 2005

Mark Hebblewhite

Douglas
Ysle of Man

Dear Mr Hebblewhite

Thank you for your letter of 10th October with reference to gloves, unfortunately you omitted to enclose your design. We look forward to receiving it in the near future.

Yours faithfully

Chloé Cassidy
P.p. B.J. Sherriff.

Mark Hebblewhite
Belmont Hill
Douglas
Isle of Man

Chloe Cassidy
BJ Sherriff International Beekeeping Supplies
Carclew Road
Mylor Downs
Falmouth
Cornwall
TR11 5UN

25th October 2005

Dear Chloe

Thanks for your letter dated 11th October. I am very sorry it has taken me a while to reply but I have been on holiday. Yes I had a good time and it was very hot, thank you. I do apologise in that I omitted to enclose my design for the new beekeeping gloves – I can only assume it was due to my excitement at both myself and Mr Sheriff making a lot of money in the near future. Please do let me know your comments on my design as I am anxious to get them into production ASAP as I have promised my wife we can get the bathroom done early in the new year and she wants some expensive taps.

Yours faithfully

Mark Hebblewhite.

Mark Hebblewhite

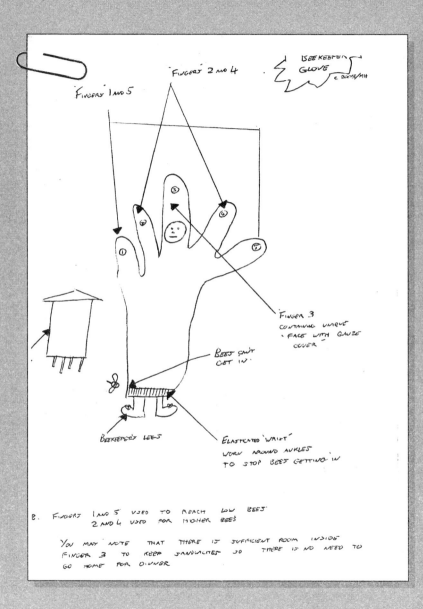

FINGERS 2 AND 4

FINGERS 1 AND 5

BEEKEEPERS GLOVE
© 2005/MH

①
②
③
④
⑤
:-)

FINGER 3
CONTAINING UNIQUE
FACE WITH GAUZE
COVER

BEES CAN'T
GET IN

BEEKEEPER'S LEGS

ELASTICATED 'WRIST'
WORN AROUND ANKLES
TO STOP BEES GETTING IN

B. FINGERS 1 AND 5 USED TO REACH LOW BEES
2 AND 4 USED FOR HIGHER BEES

YOU MAY NOTE THAT THERE IS SUFFICIENT ROOM INSIDE
FINGER 3 TO KEEP SANDWICHES SO THERE IS NO NEED TO
GO HOME FOR DINNER

Mark Hebblewhite
Belmont Hill
Douglas
Isle of Man

British Institute of Master Barbers
33 Barbourne Road
Worcester
WR1 1SA

19th December 2005

Dear Sir

I am a Gentleman Barber who would very much like to join your organisation and I would be most grateful if you would allow me to submit an application form. There is a similar organisation on the island but its head is the mayor and unfortunately we are no longer on speaking terms since I accidentally sent his son to the shop to fetch me a Kit-Kat whilst I was halfway through his tramlines (the mayor's son, not the mayor).

I would also like to enquire if your organisation has a communal pool of resources from which members are able to draw upon for inspirations as to new styles. Thank you for your assistance with this matter.

Yours sincerely

Mark Hebblewhite.

Mark Hebblewhite

Mark Hebblewhite
Belmont Hill
Douglas
Isle of Man

Wendy Cowlin
The Helicopter Museum
Locking Moor Road
Weston-Super-Mare
Somerset
BS24 8PP

19th December 2005

Dear Wendy

I wonder if you are able to assist me with this matter. As the founder member of the recently formed Isle of Man Remote Controlled Helicopter Club (IOMWJLRCH), myself and my fellow members are planning a spectacular stunt to make our mark on the island's thriving club scene.

We plan to fly our helicopters (in relay) between the island and Heysham on the 29th January 2006, weather permitting. During this stunt we will of course be stationed on the deck of the ferry, having already secured the permission of the captain. Should our attempt prove successful I would like to ask if it would be possible to send in a write-up to yourselves at the Helicopter Museum as hopefully it would be the sort of thing that the visitors to your establishment would be interested in as well as providing a little publicity for our stunt. In return for your assistance I would be more than happy to name one of the (hopefully) successfully helicopters after you (for the duration of the trip) and should you desire it we could paint your museum's logo/your face on the side of one of the participating crafts. We will be most grateful if you could support us in this endeavour.

Yours sincerely

Mark Hebblewhite.

Mark Hebblewhite

The Heliport, Weston-super-Mare, Somerset BS24 8PP, England
Tel: 01934 635227 Fax: 01934 645230
E-mail: office@helimuseum.fsnet.co.uk Web: http://www.helicoptermuseum.co.uk

Mark Hebblewhite

Douglas
Isle of Man

11th January 2006

Dear Mark

Thank you for your letter dated 19th December and apologies for the delay in replying. I have been away on holiday for the last two weeks and you know what the pre-Christmas rush is like!

In answer to your request, yes that would be fine. Some photos of the event would be great, if you can spare any.

I look forward to hearing from you and wish you lots of success on the 29th January.

Yours sincerely

Wendy

Wendy Cowlin
Manager

  Supported by the
Heritage Lottery Fund

Hon Vice Presidents: G. Blower (Italy), J. Boulet (France), Captain E.M. Brown CBE, DSC, AFC, MA, FRAeS, RN (UK), S. Sikorsky (USA), M. Tishchenko (USSR)

The British Rotorcraft Museum & Avon Air Collection Ltd, Locking Moor Road, Weston-super-Mare, Somerset, England BS24 8PP
Registered Charity No. 281053 V.A.T. Registration No. 520 1958 68 Company Registration No. 151 7593

Mark Hebblewhite
Belmont Hill
Douglas
Isle of Man

Wendy Cowlin
The Helicopter Museum
Locking Moor Road
Weston-Super-Mare
Somerset
BS24 8PP

19th January 2006

Dear Wendy

Thank you for your letter of the 11th January. We are most pleased that you and the helicopter museum are supporting our stunt. I have shown your letter to the IOMWJLRCH's other member (Isle of Man Remote Controlled Helicopter Club) and Brian is over the moon that we have some support at last. We look forward to sending you some photos and a write-up of the event which we hope that you will be able to use.

Myself and Brian hope you have had a lovely holiday. You are so lucky to be able to enjoy such an interesting job. We have just been on a holiday to the West Midlands on an industrial heritage tour which we found most gratifying. The only thing was Brian had to have a tetanus jab after slashing his ankle on a rusty nail whilst we were looking at a model of Crompton's Mule.

Best wishes

Mark

Mark

Mark Hebblewhite
Belmont Hill
Douglas
Isle of Man

Wendy Cowlin
The Helicopter Museum
Locking Moor Road
Weston-Super-Mare
Somerset
BS24 8PP
England

31st January 2006

Dear Wendy

I am both pleased and proud to announce that the IOMWJLRCH's recent helicopter flight between the Isle of Man and Heysham was completed successfully. As promised please find below a write-up of the event for your perusal. Hopefully you will be able to use it to attract visitors to your establishment.

'A wet and windy morning did not provide ideal conditions for the IOMWJLRCH's daring stunt, one which has never been attempted before and the likes of which we are never likely to see again. At 7:15am on the 29th January it was all systems go. With Mark at the controls the first leg was soon underway; the Lynx (Cowlin 2) made sterling progress in the early morning drizzle. After a circuit of the ship the Lynx was skilfully piloted to within inches of the choppy sea – dangerously close to the waves, it looked as if the craft was taunting the steel grey ocean. Onlookers gasped in admiration but the skill of the pilot ensured that there was not at any time even the slightest risk to the craft due to the experience and knowledge of the operator. Six miles out and the weather worsened. The Lynx was buffeted by icy blasts strong enough to blow a man off his feet. Somehow the operator managed to retain full control and was able to bring the craft back to the ship in time for the first changeover.

With Brian at the controls of the Sea King the changeover was smooth, but not for long. Despite a rapid and drastic improvement in the weather, keeping the craft airborne was a struggle for Brian. It is possible that a recent foot injury caused as Brian was looking at a model of Crompton's mule was the cause of the apparent lack of control – however, onlookers could not fail to notice that it seemed almost certain that disaster was about to strike. Stepping up to the helm Brian glumly handed the controls back to Mark who within seconds was able to bring the craft into line despite the weather taking a sudden turn for the worse, which had it not been for the skill of the operator, would have jeopardised the entire stunt. Somehow the Sea King was able to perform a variety of acrobatic manoeuvres including a full roll before the finale where the IOMWJLRCH's logo was written in the sky, a testament to the skill of the operator. The controls were then handed back to Brian who despite the sudden and rapid improvement in the weather had difficulty in controlling the craft.

With the final leg about to begin, the Sea King was brought back to the bridge to enable the Lynx to complete the final leg of the stunt. As the weather worsened it seemed at first as if success was out of reach. Onlookers gasped as the Lynx plummeted towards the ocean but Mark, the operator, somehow managed to bring the craft under control and was even able to perform a zig-zag manoeuvre as the English coast grew ever closer. With just a mile to go the Lynx raced ahead of the ship and after swooping low over the terminal building in Heysham the craft performed a victory lap of the ship as it came into port and landed without incident on the bridge. Never before has such a stunt been attempted and it is a credit to the IOMWJLRCH that it was pulled off.'

The IOMWJLRCH would like to thank the Helicopter Museum and in particular Wendy Cowlin for her support of the stunt. Please contact the Helicopter Museum for details of how to join the IOMWJLRCH.

Many thanks for your support in this stunt, Wendy, and I hope to hear from you soon.

Best wishes

Mark

Mark

Mark Hebblewhite
Belmont Hill
Douglas
Isle of Man

Office of Fair Trading
Fleetbank House
2-6 Salisbury Square
London
EC4Y 8JX

29th December 2006

Dear Sir

I do hope that you are able to assist me. I am the owner and operator of a small family-run newsagent and I am writing to ask for your advice and assistance in solving a dispute with a rival trader who has opened up shop just two doors down despite my objections and despite the business being in my family for over 30 years in the same location. Approximately 40% of my shop's takings can be (or rather used to be) attributed to confectionery sales e.g. Midget Gems, Wine Gums and especially liquorice Catherine wheels, which are very popular with elderly clientele. My rival is aware of this and has begun to undercut my prices thus losing me business. This week alone he had slashed individual 'flying saucers' to 2p instead of the 3p that I charge and he is giving away 'a swizzle stick' with each quarter of 'rhubarb and custards' purchased from his lower class establishment. Please can you advise me what course of action is most likely to put pay to this treachery since I have tried broaching the subject in an amiable manner but he sent his grandson in (in disguise) who then fingered all of my chocolate mice rendering them unsaleable. I do hope that you are able to assist me with this matter.

Yours sincerely

Mark Hebblewhite.

Mark Hebblewhite

Mr Mark Hebblewhite,

Douglas,
Isle of Man,

Your ref		Direct line	(020) 7211 8929
Our ref	L/48428	Fax	(020) 7211 8877
Date	06 January 2006	Email	Enquiries@oft.gov.uk

Dear Mr Hebblewhite,

Thank you for your letter to the Office of Fair Trading (OFT).

I am sorry to hear of the difficulties you have been experiencing, but unfortunately this Office is unable to help you in this instance. We do not have the power to advise on or assist with, individual traders' business disputes, as the Enterprise Act 2002 generally restricts the OFT's duties to consumer trade practices. It would appear that the matter you describe involves an alleged business to business transaction and therefore falls outside the terms of the Act. I should add that we are equally unable to intervene in individual consumer problems. On the basis of the information that you have provided, I would suggest that you might wish to consider seeking your own independent legal advice.

Thank you for drawing our attention to your problem and I hope that it will be resolved to your satisfaction in the near future.

Yours sincerely

Tom Murray
OFT Enquiries

INVESTOR IN PEOPLE

Office of Fair Trading
Fleetbank House
2-6 Salisbury Square
London EC4Y 8JX
Switchboard: (020) 7211 8000
www.oft.gov.uk

Mark Hebblewhite
Belmont Hill
Douglas
Isle of Man

Tom Murray
Enquiries
Office of Fair Trading
Fleetbank House
2-6 Salisbury Square
London
EC4Y 8JX

20th January 2006

Dear Tom

Many thanks for your letter dated the 6th January. As you kindly suggested I have taken legal advice with regard to my rival newsagent's somewhat dubious business practices but unfortunately the advice that I have been given is that I should think long and hard about taking legal recompense due to the potential cost of court cases etc. This being the case I have decided to beat him at his own game and this has proved to be a huge success. On Tuesday I arranged for a long-standing customer of mine to visit my rival's premises and put a pin prick in all of his sherbet fountains and 'salt' his fizzy cola bottles. I would like to thank you for your assistance with this matter and with your permission I will also be writing to your superiors to advise them of your consciousness and dedication to your role in support of small businessmen such as myself. I would be most grateful if you could advise me of any further actions that I could take against this upstart in order to win back my sales.

Best wishes

Mark Hebblewhite.

Mark Hebblewhite

Mark Hebblewhite
Belmont Hill
Douglas
Isle of Man

Plastic Pipe Manufacturers Society
89 Cornwall Street
Birmingham
West Midlands
B3 3BY

29th December 2005

Dear Sir

I wonder if you would be able to assist me in a project that I will be undertaking next spring which will be my first step into the world of self-sufficiency. Please can you advise me of the type of pipes I would need to install in order to irrigate a moderately sized vegetable patch? I hope to grow mostly radishes and should the scheme prove successful I have plans to expand in 2007 with a view to turnips and possibly other varieties of tubers. I would then be in a position to purchase at least 24 foot of piping. Thank you in anticipation of your assistance with this matter.

Yours sincerely

Mark Hebblewhite.

Mark Hebblewhite

PLASTIC PIPE MANUFACTURERS SOCIETY

89 CORNWALL STREET
BIRMINGHAM
B3 3BY

Telephone: 0121-236 1866
Fax: 0121-200 1389
Our Ref: GCS/16010

03 January 2006

Mr M Hebblewhite

Douglas
Isle of Man

Dear Mr Hebblewhite,

Thank you for your letter of 29 December.

I wish to inform you that as of 31 December 2005, PPMS ceased all activities and will, therefore, be unable to assist with your enquiry.

All former members of the Society are also members of the British Plastics Federation – Pipes Group. I am sure they will be able to help you with your enquiry.

Their address is:

British Plastics Federation
Plastic Pipes & Fittings Group
6 Bath Place
Rivington Street
London
EC2A 3JE

Yours sincerely

Garran Saunders
PPMS Secretary

Mark Hebblewhite
Belmont Hill
Douglas
Isle of Man

Garran Saunders
Plastic Pipe Manufacturers Society
89 Cornwall Street
Birmingham
West Midlands
B3 3BY

Ref. GCS/16010

5th January 2006

Dear Garran

Many thanks for your letter with regards to my enquiry about my vegetable patch. I am sorry to hear that the Plastic Pipe Manufacturers Society ceased its activities on the 31st December; I have not seen anything in the press about it. I thought I had better write in case you were there all on your own – I thought you might have been locked in or something if you were maybe in the toilets combing your hair when they set the alarms. Please let me know if you are OK. I hope you have all managed to secure suitably well-paid employment and that yourself and all of your colleagues had a really good leaving 'do'. To commemorate the passing of the society I have composed a short verse which I hope will assist some way towards celebrating and commemorating the good work carried out by the society prior to its unfortunate demise. I would greatly appreciate your comments on my work.

Cry not Garran Saunders
Associates and such like
A celebration, wipe those tears
Behold the plastic pipe

Looking down upon us
Just think what's in a name

Reincarnate for the grace of God
A phoenix from the flames

Don't turn your back my friend
Look skyward in celebration
Spirit of your aims reflected by
The Plastics Federation

All the very best for 2006.

Yours sincerely

Mark Hebblewhite.

Mark Hebblewhite

Mark Hebblewhite
Belmont Hill
Douglas
Isle of Man

Association of Organ Enthusiasts
Mrs Joan Gande
'Gledsdale'
416 Manchester Road
Marsden
Huddersfield
HD7 6DP

4th January 2006

Dear Joan

My partner has bought me an organ for Christmas but I am unable to get it working properly. Since she has lost the receipt the shop will not take it back and so far has only offered to examine the machine at a charge. The model is a Casio PX1 and when I turn it on and press the rhythm button it permanently plays 'bossa nova 2', i.e. it goes 'dop dop dip diddle opp dop dip' and just will not stop. I am more interested in playing classical music/easy listening and this rhythm is not at all suitable. Please can you advise me if the preset rhythm button can be bypassed in any way? Many thanks for your help with this.

Best wishes

Mark Hebblewhite.

Mark Hebblewhite

The Association of Organ Enthusiasts

55 Belle Vue, Wordsley, Stourbridge, West Midlands. DY8 5DB.
Tel: 01384 274500

Mark Hebblewhite Esq.

29th January 2006

DOUGLAS
Isle of Man

Dear Mr Hebblewhite,

Further to our brief telephone conversation today, once again we were cut off and despite re-dialling I could not get back to you, I thought it was best to drop you a line.

I was unable to find any information relating to Casio PXI, but Casio, who should be able to help if you require further information, can be contacted as follows:

Casio Customer Service Centre
Unit 6
1000 North Circular Road
London
NW2 7JD

Casio Technical Helpline   Tel: 020 8450 9131

Best Wishes,

George Ingley
Chairman
Association of Organ Enthusiasts

Mark Hebblewhite
Belmont Hill
Douglas
Isle of Man

Margaret Morris
Chairman
British Clematis Society
18 Sycamore Place
Bradwell Village
Burford
Oxon
OX18 4XG

5th January 2006

Dear Margaret

Please could you help settle a dispute for me that I am currently having with a fellow gardener? Which is the hardest, clematis or some ivy? Trevor's clematis is outside all winter and suffers no ill effects but when I bring my ivy indoors for the winter it withers. I am thinking of switching brands. Please can you help me with this?

Yours sincerely

Mark Hebblewhite.

Mark Hebblewhite

18 Sycamore Place
Bradwell Village
Burford
Oxon OX 18 4XG

10th January 2006

Dear Mark Hebblewhite

Further to your letter of the 5th, on the merits of growing clematis or ivies, *It is generally accepted that the majority of clematis are hardy* and would certainly grow well over in the Isle of man,

Ernest Marckham wrote some years ago that clematis are as hardy as old oaks, and many grow in much colder climates across northern Europe ie Sweden Northern Germany , Poland ,Estonia and Russia.

Your main problem could be the wind as the island is quiet exposed, so it may be advisable to grow them up companion plants that will give extra protection.

On the subject of Ivies, many are also hardy , and should grow well outside and not require bringing in for the winter, but you need to select the correct ones. Small ivies that are grown for summer bedding will not normally survive the winter outdoors, unless we have a mild one.

Hope this will be useful and help you to make the choice, we also enclose a set of fact sheets with information on growing clematis.

Yours sincerely

Margaret Morris

Chairman
British Clematis Society

Margaret Morris
Chairman
British Clematis Society
18 Sycamore Place
Bradwell Village
Burford
Oxon
OX18 4XG

20th January 2006

Thanks for your letter dated 10th January. I was not aware that clematisisis were as hard as you said. I have passed this information on to Trevor and I am currently in the process of following your advice and selecting some companion plants for my clematisisis. In your letter you mentioned that Ernest Markham wrote that they were as hardy as old oaks – did he actually try growing them in Estonia and Russia as it is very cold? We went once to Tallinn in Estonia and it was ever so cheap there. If Ernest really did grow them there he perhaps bought lots and lots of them to grow and only some of them survived. Who is Ernest by the way? I was once in the Boys' Brigade and our leader Mr Markham had a brother called Ernest although I think he was more interested in allotments. Many thanks for your help with my gardening.

Best wishes

Mark

Mark

British Clematis Society

18 Sycamore Place
Bradwell
Burford. Oxon
OX 18 4XG

February 9th 2006

Dear Mark

Just a short note, following your comments on the 20th Jan to say that Ernest Markham was Head Gardener at Gravety Manor in Sussex in the early 1920's and in conjunction with Jackmans of Woking helped to introduce a number of new Clematis, and had one named after himself.

So far as Estonia is concerned there is a very good nursery over there , and we have had a number of new clematis introduced over the last few years, ie Semu Tentil , and from Russia Aljonuska which won an award on our Trial grounds in 1998.

Finally just to say that the plural of Clematis is Clematis- hope this helps and that Trevor and you enjoy growing your clematis.

Kind Regards

Margaret Morris
Chairman

Encl VIRGIN BOWER — THIS IS A COPY OF ONE OF
THE FIRST clematis Books PRODUCED

Mark Hebblewhite
Belmont Hill
Douglas
Isle of Man

Margaret Morris
Chairman
British Clematis Society
18 Sycamore Place
Bradwell Village
Burford
Oxon
OX18 4XG

16th February 2006

Dear Margaret

Many thanks for your letter dated 9th February. Myself and Trevor
were over the moon with the copy of the 'The Virgin's Bower'.
I would like to make a small donation to the society in return
for your kindness and assistance if this would be possible. I had
asked Trevor to read through the book and highlight all of the
information relevant to the growing of clematis but unfortunately
Trevor did not realise the whole book was about clematisisis and
has highlighted every word. I should have perhaps asked him to
highlight any information specifically relevant to initial planting
but Trevor often takes instructions very literally. I recently asked
him to build me a duck house for the family of little chicks that
is currently living at the bottom of the garden and I asked him to
make sure they could not escape (due to problems with predators)
– however, he took this to mean that it did not require a door. I have
since modified the construction and we have planted clematisisis
to hide the chicken wire. I would be pleased to send you a diagram
of the duck house with its clematis accompaniment should you be
interested.

Best wishes

Mark

Mark

Mark Hebblewhite
Belmont Hill
Douglas
Isle of Man

Health Food Manufacturers' Association
63 Hampton Court Way
Thames Ditton
Surrey
KT7 0LT

19th January 2006

Dear Sir or Madam

I am writing to ask your advice on a new business venture I hope to undertake shortly. I have been a vegetarian for 21 years (since the age of 10) and I am currently operating my own chip van. During this time I have noticed that vegetarian customers were rarely catered for adequately and to counter this I invented my own style of vegetarian burgers. They have been hugely successful and I am currently selling over 140 per week. I was thinking of approaching frozen food manufacturers with the recipe however I am unsure of how to do this hence my letter to you. It would be great if you could give me some advice on the subject. Also my product is called 'Mark's Nutty Nut Nut Burgers' and I am keen to protect this name in the event of my rivals adopting it for their products. Many thanks for your assistance with this matter and I hope to hear from you soon.

Kind regards

Mark Hebblewhite.

Mark Hebblewhite

HEALTH FOOD MANUFACTURERS' ASSOCIATION

Director: David Adams, 63 Hampton Court Way, Thames Ditton, Surrey KT7 0LT
Telephone: 0208 398 4066 Facsimile: 0208 398 5402
Email: d.adams@hfma.co.uk, Web site: http://www.hfma.co.uk

Mark. Hebblewhite

Douglas
Isle of Man

23.01.06

Dear Mark,

Thank you for your letter dated 19th January, regarding your new business venture.

May I suggest you contact your local chamber of commerce on information on setting up your business and the Patent Office to apply for a trade Mark (www.patent.gov.uk)

I hope this helps and wish you all the best in your new venture.

Yours Sincerely

Linda Philips
Office Manager

VAT No. 233 6384 65

Mark Hebblewhite
Belmont Hill
Douglas
Isle of Man

Linda Phillips
Health Food Manufacturers' Association
63 Hampton Court Way
Thames Ditton
Surrey
KT7 0LT

29th January 2006

Dear Linda

Thank you for your reply dated 23rd January with regard to my new and innovative product – Mark's Nutty Nut Nut Burgers. I have taken your advice and applied for a trademark. In return for your assistance I am pleased to offer you some vouchers for a free Nutty Nut Nut Burger for yourself and your colleagues. If you let me know the number you require I will get them in the post for you as soon as possible. I also have one further request you may be able to help me with. As an entrepreneur I am constantly striving to improve my product and to that end would it be possible to ask everyone in the office what their favourite nuts are. Please place a tick under the preferred nut/kernel.

Employee Walnut Brazil Hazelnut Pine Cashew Other

1
2
3
4
5
6
7
8
9
10

Many thanks for your help with this.

Mark Hebblewhite.

Mark Hebblewhite

Mark Hebblewhite
Belmont Hill
Douglas
Isle of Man

Keith Vincent
The Jaguar Enthusiasts Club
Abbeywood Office Park
Emma Chris Way
Filton
Bristol
BS34 7JU

2nd February 2006

Dear Keith

I found your address on www.bigcats.com and I am writing to offer to adopt Mr Bojangles. My wife and I are able to contribute a maximum of £40 per month in order to keep him well fed and vaccinated. Like yourselves we are great admirers of these diurnal hunters. If possible I would like to know whether or not this would be possible as it is our gold wedding anniversary and I would like to surprise her.

Best wishes

Mark Hebblewhite.

Mark Hebblewhite

17th February 2006

Dear Mr. Hebblewhite,

Thank you for your letter, unfortunately there appears to be a misunderstanding. The Jaguar Enthusiasts Club is for lovers of the Motor Car not the Big cat.

Whilst I agree with you these animals must be saved we are not connected in any way with a means of sending them money. I'm not sure how are address was on this website. I have checked and cannot find it there.

Yours sincerely

Tel: 0117 969 8186
Fax: 0117 979 1863

e-mail: graham.searle@btinternet.com

Graham Searle
General Manager

Jaguar Enthusiasts Club Limited. Website: www.jec.org.uk Office email: jechq@btopenworld.com
Registered Office: Abbeywood Office Park, Emma Chris Way, Filton, South Gloucestershire BS34 7JU
Registered in England No. 2051456 VAT Registration No. 413 4058 86

 Jaguar
Enthusiasts
Club Racing

 Jaguar
Enthusiasts
Club Travel

JEC
DIRECT

 Members of the
Federation of British
Historic Vehicle Clubs

Mark Hebblewhite
Belmont Hill
Douglas
Isle of Man

Mr G Searle
The Jaguar Enthusiasts Club
Abbeywood Office Park
Emma Chris Way
Filton
Bristol
BS34 7JU

27th February 2006

Dear Graham

Thank you for your letter dated 17th February. I can only apologise for troubling you with my request to assist Mr Bojangles. I will be writing to The Jaguar Enthusiasts Club (the Big Cats one) to suggest they include the word cat in the name of their organisation to clarify the matter further and avoid unnecessary confusion. I am pleased to let you know that I have at last been able to make a contribution towards the upkeep of Mr Bojangles and all is well. Lastly could I enquire if your organisation has a newsletter? It has occurred to me that members of your club might be interested in joining the Jaguar Enthusiasts Club of which I am now a member (the Big Cats one). Any of your members that are interested could contact me for an application form and in return I will attempt to recruit members from my club that have an interest in Jaguars (your club). I feel that a mutual alliance could benefit both clubs. Please let me know if it would be possible for your organisation to assist me in this way with an article in your newsletter.

Yours sincerely

Mark Hebblewhite.

Mark Hebblewhite

Mark Hebblewhite
Belmont Hill
Douglas
Isle of Man

Scottish Fencing
589 Lanark Road
Edinburgh
EH14 5DA

13th February 2006

Dear Mr McTavish/Miss Catfish

I have been passed your address by Steve from ABC Building Services who said that you would be able to assist me. I would very much appreciate it if you could advise me where I can purchase a cat-proof fence in order that these pests are not able to dig up my borders. We currently have a large scare-cat device in the garden but the beasts seem to have grown used to it and have become daring enough to scratch its securing bracket. We have also tried all the other usual remedies such as hosepipes but to no avail. We are not looking for a fence that would in any way be harmful to these beasts, merely to exclude their access to our property. In addition to this the fence must be strong enough to withstand high winds as we live on a corner. Many thanks in anticipation of your assistance with this matter.

Yours sincerely

Mark Hebblewhite.

Mark Hebblewhite

Scottish Fencing Ltd

(a company limited by guarantee)

589 Lanark Road, Edinburgh, EH14 5DA

Tel. 0131 453 9074, Fax 0131 453 9079
email: **scottishfencing@aol.com** , web: www.scottish-fencing.com

sportscotland

Mr Mark Hebblewhite

Douglas
Isle of Man

22 February 2006

Dear Mr Hebblewhite,

Re your letter, dated 13 February, enquiring about a cat-proof fence: I must inform you that we appear to have a case of mistaken identity. Scottish Fencing Ltd is the governing body in Scotland for the modern sport of fencing; we are in no way involved in the provision of garden defences against cats; indeed, any attempt to make use of swords for that purpose would be likely to attract the attention of the RSPCA.

May I wish you success in your quest elsewhere?

Yours sincerely,

Alan Loveland .

Alan Loveland
Temporary Executive Administrator

Registered Office: 1 Rutland Court, Edinburgh, Midlothian, EH3 8EY.   Company No.:SC265956

Mark Hebblewhite
Belmont Hill
Douglas
Isle of Man

Alan Loveland
Scottish Fencing
589 Lanark Road
Edinburgh
EH14 5DA

2nd March 2006

Dear Mr Alan

On Guard!

I can only apologise for my letter dated 13th Feb in which I attempted to seek your assistance in restricting feline access to my garden. As you described in your letter it was a case of mistaken identity on my behalf and for that I doff my cap and tug at my forelock with a great deal of effort. I am now aware that your organisation does not supply garden defences to exclude cats and I would like to reassure you that in no way would I attempt to prevent these beasts accessing my property with the use of a rapier. I feel this would be immoral since in the UK at least cats are unskilled in the art of duelling and to my knowledge there is not at present a head shield on the market that could accommodate their ears. Perhaps this is an opportunity we can explore. I have recently read that there are approximately 9 million extreme cat lovers in the UK (not including Sheffield and the district of North Kesteven) who might perhaps like to steer their beasts towards this most gentlemanly of sports.

I look forward to hearing your comments on my idea and I hope to hear from you soon.

Touché

Mark Hebblewhite.

Mark Hebblewhite

Mark Hebblewhite
Belmont Hill
Douglas
Isle of Man

British Footwear Association
3 Burystead Place
Wellingborough
Northants
NN8 1AH

13th February 2006

Dear Sir

I wonder if your organisation would be able to assist me in a venture that I am undertaking. To give you a little history I have been a shoe retailer for 18 years and during that time for one reason or another I have accumulated over 700 single shoes. I am assuming that the reasons for this are as follows:

1)   They were delivered to myself and they were not checked in properly
2)   People have purchased odd pairs/styles

As far as I am aware this is a common problem in the shoe retailing industry and to that end for many years I have been seeking a solution. One semi-successful strategy I have adopted is to put all my 'odds' into piles, i.e. all black right size 10's together, all black left size 10's together, and try to make up as many pairs that look as close to each other as possible, fasten them together with cable ties, and get half price for them from less fashion conscious members of the community or perhaps people whose work does not bring them into everyday contact with people, i.e. dog wardens. To get to my point the other day I received an email from a long-lost work colleague through Friends Reunited – he had worked with me back in the 1970s when we were both part-timers in a 'weigh and save' type shop.

My idea is simple, Sir – www.shoematch.com. For a nominal charge of say £60 per month shoe retailers would be able to enter the details of their 'odds' onto a national database and perform a search for the missing shoe or mule etc. I estimate that this will save the industry thousands each year. As the primary footwear association I would be interested to hear your thoughts on my idea and should you like it perhaps we could take the idea forward together.

Yours sincerely

Mark Hebblewhite.

Mark Hebblewhite

british footwear association ltd

3 Burystead Place
Wellingborough
Northants NN8 1AH

Tel: +44 (0) 1933 229005
Fax: +44 (0) 1933 225009

E-mail: info@britfoot.com
Website: www.britfoot.com

20 March 2006

Mark Hebblewhite

Douglas
Isle of Man

Dear Mr Hebblewhite

Thanks for your letter about odd shoes. I did not realise that this was such a common problem and in fact we are more conscious of the reverse ie consumers wanting to buy odd shoes. Clarks have apparently recently suspended their odd shoe service. There is a charity – Solemates – for people who need odd shoes and you might like to contact them as a possible outlet for some of your odd shoes. Their contact details are:

> Solemates
> 46 Gordon Road
> Chingford
> London
> E4 6BU
> Tel: 0208 524 2423

We will put a note about your shoe match idea in the next IFRA newsletter. This reaches hundreds of independent footwear retailers and we will see what reaction it generates.

Yours sincerely

Niall Campbell

Niall Campbell
<u>Chief Executive</u>

Cc Caroline Bean

Marketing enquiries: 5 Portland Place London W1B 1PW Tel: +44 (0) 20 7580 8687 Fax: +44 (0) 20 7580 8696 E-mail: marketing@britfoot.com

British Footwear Association is a company limited by guarantee registered in England (No 59737) at 5 Portland Place London W1B 1PW

Mark Hebblewhite
Belmont Hill
Douglas
Isle of Man

Niall Campbell
British Footwear Association
3 Burystead Place
Wellingborough
Northants
NN8 1AH

21st March 2006

Dear Mr Campbell

Many thanks for your response to my letter about the problems I have been experiencing in my shoe shop. I am greatly encouraged by your positive feedback on my website idea and it would be great to get some feedback from the industry when my idea is mentioned in your newsletter. Would it be possible to ask if you would be prepared to send me a copy of the newsletter once my idea is 'rolled out' to the industry? I ask because I am not presently a member of your organisation and have never seen a copy of your newsletter. Nor am I likely to be able to afford to join until I have dealt with my problem 'odds'. On a brighter note thank you for your suggestion to contact Solemates; I was not aware that such an odd shoe charity existed. I will be writing to them forthwith to offer them all the 'odds' I have not been able to sell on. Since my original letter on the 13th February I have managed to reduce my odd shoes from 750 to 428 although this figure does not include mules nor flip-flops. This is mainly due to the National Dog Warden Association who have agreed to take 100 pairs at £1/pair for their new recruits. Thank you for your assistance with my idea and I hope to hear from you soon.

Yours sincerely

Mark Hebblewhite.

Mark Hebblewhite

Mark Hebblewhite
Belmont Hill
Douglas
Isle of Man

Solemates
46 Gordon Road
Chingford
London
E4 6BU

15th April 2006

Dear Sir/Madam

I have been passed your address by Niall Campbell, Chief Executive of the British Footwear Association, who said that you might like some of my 'odd' shoes that I have come across after having a clearout at work.

I am in possession of 428 at present not including flip-flops or mules. The National Dog Warden Association has taken 100 off me so far for their new recruits. I have a list of all the shoes if you'd like me to forward it for your perusal. It is comprised of 126 brogues, 57 assorted trainers, 115 boots, 117 dress shoes, 1 snowboarding boot, 1 thigh length boot, 1 steel toecap shoe and 1 cherry red Doc Marten. I would very much like you to take these shoes off my hands. They are not actually on my hands, hence there is no rush, but I would hate them to go to waste.

Yours sincerely

Mark Hebblewhite.

Mark Hebblewhite

Mark Hebblewhite
Belmont Hill
Douglas
Isle of Man

Tim Harris
Animal Transportation Association
PO BOX 251
Redhill
RH1 5FU

27th February 2006

Dear Tim

I have been passed your address by Reverend Beasley of Whitley Bay Photographic Society who suggested you as my first point of contact after you assisted him last year with the problems he experienced with his herd of Laughton lamb and turnips outside 'The Archibald Knox'. I do hope you will be able to provide me with some guidance as to regulations governing the capturing of images of animals during movement to and fro, without the use of filters or harnesses, but present on a moving motor vehicle travelling within the legal speed limit. I would be grateful if you could advise me and contact both myself and Rev Beasley with your advice. Rev Beasley can be contacted through

Mrs Jan Clements
Whitley Bay Photographic Society
31 St Mary's Avenue
Whitley Bay
Tyne and Wear

I would also be grateful if you could forward me a copy of your reply to Reverend Beasley/Jan Clements for my records.

I look forward to hearing from you.

Kindest regards

Mark Hebblewhite.

Mark Hebblewhite

AATA - Animal Transportation Association

European Office
PO Box 251
REDHILL RH1 5FU

Tel: +44 (0)1737 822249
Fax: +44 (0)1737 822954
harrisassociates@btconnect.com

02 March 2006

Mark Hebblewhite

Douglas
Isle of Man

Dear Mark

You give no phone number to call you back. I am entirely baffled by your letter.

I regret I do not know any Reverend Beasley, nor Jan Clements, nor Whitley Bay photographic society, Loughton lambs nor the turnips referred to. I have never heard of 'The Archibald Knox', which I take to be a pub, nor know where it is [sadly].

Although I am a specialist on all aspects of animal transport, I am not an expert at photographing animals in motion.

If the Reverend Beasley could enlighten me with further details I would be very pleased.

I'm really sorry that I am unable to assist.

Yours sincerely

Tim Harris SDA
European Secretary, AATA;
Editor and Publisher of the *AATA Manual for the Transportation of Animals*

AATA - Animal Transportation Association

European Office
PO Box 251
REDHILL RH1 5FU

Tel: +44 (0)1737 822249
Fax: +44 (0)1737 822954
harrisassociates@btconnect.com

13 March 2006

Mark Hebblewhite

Douglas
Isle of Man

Dear Mark

I read your letter with interest, but with deepening anxiety about my failing memory. None of the names you mention are familiar to me, and I have searched my 16,000 address database. However, your last line mentions 'sleeves' which triggers a tiny grey cell.

There was an occasion long ago when I had a phone call, as I do daily, from some unnamed person asking about 'lamb sleeves'. As I remember, a female voice. It appears that she meant 'coats' that are sometimes put on lambs after birth simply to keep them dry and therefore warmer in the rain. The simplest form is merely a supermarket plastic bag with appropriate holes for the legs. Not very elegant, but it works.

These coats are now produced commercially, and the original suppliers used to be Alfred Cox though they may not stock them now:
    Alfred Cox Surgical Ltd
    Edward Road
    Coulsdon Surrey   CR3 2XA
020 8668 2131

I seem to remember putting the caller in touch with my sheep expert, John Bartelous:
    Peasridge Sheep Services Ltd
    Stonelink - Stubb Lane
    Brede Rye   Sussex TN31 6BL
01424 882900

You also mention 'your project' but don't explain what this is. Although I am writing to you as secretary of the AATA, my interests extend to any aspect of animal welfare, so I am sure I would be interested to know more about the project.

Yours sincerely

Tim Harris SDA
European Secretary, AATA;
Editor and Publisher of the _AATA Manual for the Transportation of Animals_

Mark Hebblewhite
Belmont Hill
Douglas
Isle of Man

Tim Harris
Animal Transportation Association
PO BOX 251
Redhill
RH1 5FU

22nd March 2006

Dear Tim

I thank you for your prompt response to my letter dated 8th March in the year of our Lord 2006. After a brief exchange of letters with Nichola from the Wessex Ferret Club I am able to put your mind at rest and tell you that you no long hath nay need to become anxious about losing your memory as it was the said Nichola that called you regarding lamb's sleeves/coats whilst she was wearing her other hat. I am most pleased that you are interested in animal welfare as are our good selves and I would be pleased to clear up a few details regarding our project as you requested in your letter of 13th March. Phase 2 was completed Wednesday last as anticipated although there were a number of unexpected delays due to underestimating the initial number of buckets required and the use of an inferior quality masking tape. That said the day proved to be an enormous success marred only by the inclement weather conditions at Briantspuddle. The van has now been designed and a prototype is under construction. Despite the problems of space allocation with the documentation storage area there is still more than enough room for the periscope although we are anticipating some trouble with the sun visor touching the wheels whilst moving at speed.

Yours sincerely

Mark Hebblewhite.

Mark Hebblewhite

Mark Hebblewhite
Belmont Hill
Douglas
Isle of Man

Mrs Jan Clements
Whitley Bay Photographic Society
31 St Mary's Avenue
Whitley Bay
Tyne and Wear

27th February 2006

Dear Jan

I have been passed your address by Reverend Beasley from the Animal Transportation Association who said that you may be interested in a project I am undertaking. Like yourself I am a keen photographer although I must admit that my speciality is taking pictures of famous celebrities. So far I have managed to photograph a number of famous people including Nigel Baker from the goth rock band Avalon Doom Church. Anyway, to get to the point of my letter I do hope you will be able to provide me with some guidance as to regulations governing the capturing of images of animals during movement to and fro without the use of filters or harnesses but present on a moving motor vehicle travelling within the legal speed limit. I would be grateful if you could advise me and contact both myself and Rev Beasley with your advice. Rev Beasley can be contacted through

Tim Harris
Animal Transportation Association
PO Box 251
Redhill
RH1 5FU

I would also be grateful if you could forward me a copy of your letter to Reverend Beasley/Tim Harris for my records.

Best wishes

Mark Hebblewhite.

Mark Hebblewhite

Mark Hebblewhite
Belmont Hill
Douglas
Isle of Man

The Arts Council
Manchester House
22 Bridge Street
Manchester
M3 3AB

20th March 2006

Dear Sir/Madam

I am writing with a proposal for a new and exciting play written by myself and I would very much like the support of your organisation. It is based upon the life of the great man Oscar Schindler before his fantastic achievements during World War 2. The storyline is intended to take the audience on a journey through the troubled childhood of Oscar up until his 21st birthday. Whilst a great many people are aware of the details and events in the latter part of Schindler's life, very few people are aware that for the vast majority of his early life he suffered from a debilitating speech impediment. My play is entitled 'Schindler's Lisp' and it is ready to perform as soon as I can find a suitable venue and funding with which to purchase refreshments for my troupe, hence my letter to your good self. I completed the final castings last week and my troupe is now ready and waiting to perform to the masses and beyond. I do hope you will be able to give some consideration to this project and I look forward to your response.

Yours sincerely

Mark Hebblewhite.

Mark Hebblewhite

23 March 2006

Mark Hebblewhite

Douglas
Isle of Man

Dear Mark Hebblewhite

Thank you for your letter dated 20 March 2006, with regards to your new and exciting project.

Unfortunately the Isle of Man is not an area that Arts Council England covers, I realise this is disappointing news, however I can advise that Isle of Man Arts Council offers 'support in the form of bursaries and grants to assist groups and individuals to travel off-Island to perform or take part in workshops to build on existing skills'.

Should you require information about the bursaries and Grants they offer, please visit their website: **www.gov.im/artscouncil/**, which will be able to provide information.

May I wish you every success for the future.

Yours sincerely

Jane Davis
Grants Administrator
Grant Management Unit
0161 827 9229

Arts Council England, North West, Manchester House, 22 Bridge Street, Manchester M3 3AB www.artscouncil.org.uk
Phone: 0845 300 6200 Fax: 44 (0)161 834 6969 Textphone: 44 (0)161 834 9131

Arts Council England is the trading name for The Arts Council of England. Registered charity no 1036733

Mark Hebblewhite
Belmont Hill
Douglas
Isle of Man
Isle of Man
Isle of Man
Isle of Man
Isle of Man

Jane Davis
Grants Administrator
Grants Department
The Arts Council
Manchester House
22 Bridge Street
Manchester
M3 3AB

16th April 2006

Dear Jane

Thank you for your letter dated 23rd March. Sorry it has taken me a while to reply but I have been very busy doing little odd jobs. My driveway is now clear of weeds and the shed has a new roof. You will note that I have repeated part of my address four times (above); this is because your address is bigger than mine and I enjoy the look of a letter more when it is symmetrical. I am sorry you are not able to fund my play and feed the actors. I have already approached the Isle of Man Arts Council for funding but I have been declined as technically I am not a resident yet. Please, Jane, is there any way you could bend the rules just a little? I have been to Manchester in the past and I used to live in Preston for a number of years and often fondly recall 'The Happy Haddock'. In return for your assistance I could set you up on a date with my leading actor – he has a club foot but is very handsome facially.

Happy funding

Mark Hebblewhite.

Mark Hebblewhite

Mark Hebblewhite
Belmont Hill
Douglas
Isle of Man

The Vegetarian Society of the United Kingdom
Parkdale
Dunham Road
Altrincham
Cheshire
WA14 4QG

14th March 2006

Dear Sir or Madam

I have been passed your address by the manager of my local Greens health food store and I am delighted to have discovered your organisation. Like yourselves I am a successful professional and currently I am running my own chip van/booty wagon providing the community with delightful inexpensive vegetarian food. I would be grateful if you could advise me of the correct procedure in order for me to apply for membership of your organisation. I look forward to hearing from you and may it be a long and prosperous year for you all at the association.

With very best wishes

Mark Hebblewhite.

Mark Hebblewhite

27th March 2006

VSUK TRADING LIMITED

Mark Hebblewhite

Douglas
Isle Of Man

Dear Mark

Thank you for enquiring about The Vegetarian Society Food & Drink Guild scheme. With over 5% of the UK population choosing to be strictly vegetarian and over 44% cutting down on their consumption of meat, demand for vegetarian food choice has never been stronger. Any caterer or restaurateur who can offer more than vegetarian lasagne has a clear advantage over the competition.

The Vegetarian Society can help professional caterers to take advantage of this buoyant market. Our prestigious Food & Drink Guild is the scheme under which we approve the vegetarian menus of caterers. Providing a caterer complies with our high standards and stringent criteria they can use our seedling symbol trademark to promote their vegetarian options.

We have recently worked with the NHS on their new hospital food initiative, not to mention many private restaurants, hotels and guesthouses to help develop their vegetarian choices. This has of course culminated in them being granted the use of The Vegetarian Society's prestigious mark of approval, the seedling symbol.

To ensure your business isn't missing out on potential customers from this growing sector, I enclose a copy of our Food & Drink Guild information pack which gives a detailed insight into the scheme and other business opportunities with The Vegetarian Society.

We look forward to working with you to promote your business.

Yours sincerely

Jane O'Leary
Business Development Officer

VSUK Trading Limited, Registered Company No.2120220 is a wholly owned subsidiary of
The Vegetarian Society of the United Kingdom Limited
Registered Charity No.259358 Registered Company No.959115

Parkdale Dunham Road Altrincham Cheshire WA14 4QG

INVESTOR IN PEOPLE   Tel: 0161 925 2000 Fax: 0161 926 9182 email: seedling@vegsoc.org www.vegsoc.org   Recycled Paper

Mark Hebblewhite
Belmont Hill
Douglas
Isle of Man

Jane O'Leary
The Vegetarian Society
Parkdale
Dunham Road
Altrincham
Cheshire
WA14 4QG

3rd April 2006

Dear Jane

Thank you for your letter dated 27th March inviting me to join the society. Thank you also for the information you sent on food preparation methods. I am unsure as to whether or not my own preparation techniques meet the standards set by the society – please can you advise me. I have asked my wife and she thinks they are fine – however, I would like some clarification. When I am making a lasagne to sell from my van, for reasons of economy in cooking I make one half of it vegetarian (aubergines, onions, mushrooms and spinach) and the other half with mince. When serving a vegetarian customer I use a different spoon and I am always careful to pick out any bits from the meat side that may have crossed over during the cooking process and vice versa for meat-eating customers who I might offend with the spinach. I have not had any complaints at all from customers who think my recipe is delicious. There has been the odd occasion where a small piece of mince has found its way into the vegetarian side of the dish but when it is mushed up a bit it is very difficult to tell the difference. Please can you let me know if my prep/cooking techniques need adapting or are they fine as they are? Many thanks for your assistance.

Yours sincerely

Mark Hebblewhite.

Mark Hebblewhite

Mark Hebblewhite
Belmont Hill
Douglas
Isle of Man

Benders Disposables
Solar House
282 Chase Road
London
N14 6NQ

15th March 2006

Dear Mr Bender

I have harboured a keen interest in disposable products for a number of years now and undoubtedly they are the way of the future. My favourite items include razors and tin foil trays that can be used for cooking turkeys and/or roast potatoes. A friend of mine who works in a cheese packing plant has recently told me about your organisation and I felt compelled to write and offer my encouragement and to congratulate you on your contribution to the economy in the UK.

I would like to suggest a short verse that you may feel is suitable for adoption by your organisation. It is loosely based on the Senegalese national anthem but having been adapted by myself I feel it conveys the spirit of the aims of your organisation.

Everyone strum your koras
Strike the bafalons
The red lion has roared once more
The tamer of the brush with one leap
Has scattered the gloom
Out and yet not

I would be most grateful for your comments on this verse which I hope you will be able to adopt and I look forward to hearing from you shortly.

Yours sincerely

Mark Hebblewhite.

Mark Hebblewhite

28th March 2006
ap/jj

Mark Hebblewhite

Douglas
Isle of Man

F. Bender Limited
Solar House
282 Chase Road
London
N14 6NQ
United Kingdom
Tel: +44(0) 20 8882 5252
Fax: +44(0) 20 8886 5515

e-mail:
info@benders.co.uk

Web site
www.benders.co.uk

Dear Mr Hebblewhite

Thank you for your letter showing an interest in our Company, and also congratulating us on our contribution to the economy in the UK.

The verse you so kindly adopted, although very interesting, doesn't portray our image as a manufacturer of disposable tableware.

I would like to thank you most sincerely for your enthusiasm, and wish you well for the future.

Yours sincerely
for F Bender Limited

Janet Johnson
PA to Chairman

Registered Office:
Gresford Industrial Park
Chester Road
Wrexham LL12 8LX
Registered in England & Wales
No. 1816910

BENDERS
CATERING FOR PROFESSIONALS

Mark Hebblewhite
Belmont Hill
Douglas
Isle of Man

Janet Johnson
PA to Mr Bender
F. Bender Limited
Solar House
282 Chase Road
London
N14 6NQ

3rd April 2006

Dear Janet

Many thanks for your letter dated 28th March. Although it is printed on a disposable resource I have not thrown it away! I shall be keeping it for my files. I am sorry you did not enjoy the verse I adapted for your organisation although in hindsight I can appreciate that it could be a little misleading to your customers who do not use bafalons for religious reasons. By way of apology for my inappropriate adaptation I have just this morning penned a new poem that I hope you will consider to be a much more fitting tribute to the good work carried out by all those at Benders Disposables. You will note that the typeface in heavy lettering should be sung by a male and the lighter coloured typeface by a female. It follows that I envisage the verse performed by a famous male/female duo, for example Milli Vanilli or Hank Marvin.

Why throw away?
It's quick, it's cheap
Benders value
It's unique!

Napkins, forks, spoons, and knives
A single use for an easier life
If you're having a party we've just the thing
Don't delay, give Benders a ring

Zero two **zero** eight **eight** eight **two** five **two** five **two** (with echo)
We've got just the thing for you
From a paper plate to a plastic cup
And best of all there's no washing up
We hate washing up (together)

Yours sincerely

Mark Hebblewhite.

Mark Hebblewhite

Mark Hebblewhite
Belmont Hill
Douglas
Isle of Man

The Coal Authority
200 Lichfield Lane
Mansfield
Nottinghamshire
NG18 4RG

17th March 2006

Dear Sir

As you are aware there are still substantial fossil fuel reserves in the United Kingdom but mining costs using present techniques mean that at this moment in time there is not a practical or economic way to maximise these reserves. I have been giving a great deal of thought recently to ways in which the extraction of the substantial but as yet untapped reserves of coal can be separated and extracted and after a series of experiments over the last 7 years I believe I have developed an economically viable technique that would enable this valuable resource to be exploited. With this in mind would you be interested in attending a demonstration of my methods that I hope can be used to prolong the mining industry in the UK? In order to perform a demonstration I would require access to an existing coal face with reserves that are at present not economic to mine. I do hope you are able to assist with this project.

Yours sincerely

Mark Hebblewhite.

Mark Hebblewhite

THE COAL AUTHORITY

INVESTOR IN PEOPLE

200 Lichfield Lane
Mansfield
Nottinghamshire
NG18 4RG
Tel: 01623 638250 (Direct)
       01623 427162 (Switchboard)
Fax: 01623 427316
Email: johndelaney@coal.gov.uk

John Delaney
Corporate Affairs Manager

Our Ref: CA28/3/1
Your Ref:

30 March 2006

Mark Hebblewhite,

Douglas,
Isle of Man.

Dear Mr. Hebblewhite,

Thank you for your letter of 17 March.

As the owner of the unworked coal and mines of coal in the United Kingdom, the Authority is always interested in new techniques to economically exploit the nation's coal resource. The Authority itself is prohibited from mining or exploring for coal but is the regulatory body that licenses private coal mine operators.

To enable the Authority to facilitate meaningful discussions to take place with organisations that could assist you in trialling and possibly developing your technique, I would be grateful if you could supply more detailed information on this technology.

I look forward to your response.

Yours sincerely,

John Delaney
Corporate Affairs Manager

Mark Hebblewhite
Belmont Hill
Douglas
Isle of Man

Strictly Private and Confidential
John Delaney
The Coal Authority
200 Lichfield Lane
Mansfield
Nottinghamshire
NG18 4RG

3rd April 2006

Dear John

Many thanks for your letter dated 30th March with reference to my technique to exploit the nation's coal resource. Please find enclosed a copy of a diagram outlining my methods. I trust you will find this self explanatory. I would be extremely grateful if you could arrange to put me in touch with organisations that could assist in trialling my techniques. Could you please also advise me of the application procedure in order that I can gain a licence to mine and also of the relevant costs that this will entail. I have been informed that these are available at the Post Office providing I can prove my identity.

I look forward to hearing your comments on my methods and I hope to hear from you soon.

Best wishes

Mark Hebblewhite.

Mark Hebblewhite

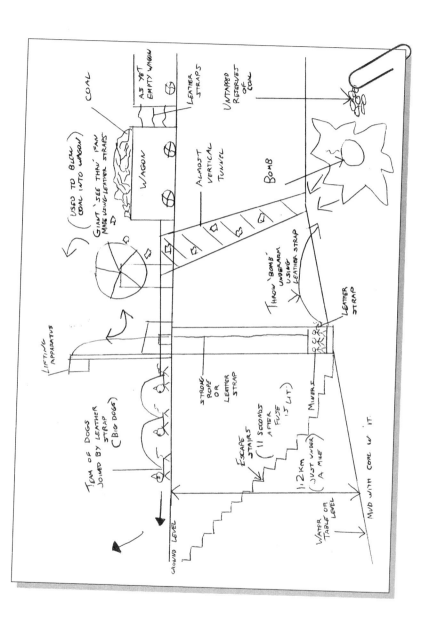

THE COAL AUTHORITY

INVESTOR IN PEOPLE

200 Lichfield Lane
Mansfield
Nottinghamshire
NG18 4RG
Tel: 01623 638250 (Direct)
        01623 427162 (Switchboard)
Fax: 01623 427316
Email: johndelaney@coal.gov.uk

John Delaney
Corporate Affairs Manager

Our Ref: CA28/3/1
Your Ref:

12 April 2006

Mark Hebblewhite,

Douglas,
Isle of Man.

Dear Mark,

Thank you for your letter of 3 April to which you attached a diagram to explain your techniques for exploiting the nation's coal resource.

To adopt a system for underground coal extraction as described in your diagram you would first need to meet the legal requirements as set out in the relevant health and safety and mines and quarries legislation. I would therefore suggest that you make contact with HM Mines Inspectorate within the Health and Safety Executive to discuss your proposed method of mining. The HSE can be contacted as follows:-

> Health and Safety Executive
> HM Inspectorate of Mines
> Edgar Allen House
> 241 Glossop Road
> Sheffield
> S10 2GW
> Tel: 0114 291 2390

Yours sincerely,

p.p. **John Delaney**
Corporate Affairs Manager

Mark Hebblewhite
Belmont Hill
Douglas
Isle of Man

John Delaney
The Coal Authority
200 Lichfield Lane
Mansfield
Nottinghamshire
NG18 4RG

16th April 2006

Dear John

Thank you for your letter with regard to my mining technique. I was not expecting such a swift response so it just goes to show that Basil's wife in the newsagent's/general store was wrong when she said that modern organisations no longer have the personal touch. She was very wrong and I will make sure she is aware of this next time I visit the establishment for my Midget Gems. I shall be writing to Her Majesty's Inspectorate of Mines with my proposal as you so kindly suggested and with any luck once approval has been granted we shall be able to resume contact and (with your assistance) trial the project. On a final note have you seen Basil's window displays? There is a sort of plinth with a bottle of washing up liquid on top (covered in dust), eight bottles of Panda cola in a line to the right of the plinth, and a selection of adhesive products in a fan type arrangement. Once again thank you for your help with my project and I look forward to working with you in the future.

Kindest regards

Mark Hebblewhite.

Mark Hebblewhite

PS – I am thinking of moving house and this being the case I am not replacing matching mugs as they are smashed. Does your organisation have any that you would be able to forward me? I shall of course ensure you are compensated.

Mark Hebblewhite
Belmont Hill
Douglas
Isle of Man

Health and Safety Executive
HM Inspectorate of Mines
Edgar Allen House
241 Glossop Road
Sheffield
S10 2GW

26th April 2006

Dear Sir or Madam

I have been passed your contact details by John Delaney, Corporate Affairs Manager at the Coal Authority, who said you may be able to assist in the new system for underground coal extraction that I have developed. The System has only been trialled on a very small scale so far but if you can give my method the all clear Mr Delaney has promised to attempt to facilitate discussions with organisations that might be interested in a large scale test of my methods. Please would it be possible to send you the relevant information with a view to your cooperation in getting this project off the ground?

Yours sincerely

Mark Hebblewhite.

Mark Hebblewhite

HSE

Health and Safety
Executive

Chief Inspector of Mines :Mr D Mitchell

Mr M Hebblewhite

Douglas
Isle of Man

Your reference:

Our reference: IW/JMP

Dear Mr Hebblewhite   Date : 5 May 2006

Thank you for your letter dated 26 April 2006 concerning a new system for underground coal extraction.

Your letter did not have a telephone contact number or I would have spoken to you directly.

The Health and Safety Executive is the regulator for the Mining Industries and I have no direct role in the assessment or development of new production systems. I do however have clear interests in the development of new technologies from a safety and health viewpoint and I am in direct contact with the various sectors of the mining industries.

I would be happy to see more of your proposal and I could discuss with you if you see that as of value. My telephone and e-mail contacts are at the foot of this letter and I would be pleased to hear from you.

Yours sincerely

I WAUGH
HM Principal District Inspector of Mines
ian.waugh@hse.gsi.gov.uk

HM Inspectorate of Mines
Edgar Allen House, 241 Glossop Road,, Sheffield S10 2GW
☎ 0114 291 2390 📠 0114 291 2399 ⌨

Mark Hebblewhite
Belmont Hill
Douglas
Isle of Man

Frances Gillick
The Department of Health
Corporate Human Resources
Room 286d
Skipton House
80 London Road
London
SE1 6LH

12th April 2006

Dear Frances

I would like to apply for the post of Director General – workforce as advertised in the Sunday Times on 9th April 2006. I have never had a day off sick since 1996 when I got a fishbone stuck in my throat.

I am committed to the objectives laid out by your organisation and in my mind I possess proven strategic HR leadership skills. When I worked in a warehouse I once heard Colin call someone a poof and I said it was wrong straight away but they still picked me up by my arms and legs and banged my head into the rack where the cheap T-shirts were kept. I would be grateful if you could forward details of my approximate starting date. I need to be off on 26th July as I am going to a party in Nottingham.

Yours sincerely

Mark Hebblewhite.

Mark Hebblewhite

Department
of Health

Skipton House
80 London Road
London
SE1 6LH

Tel: 020 7972 2000
Direct Line: 020 7972

Dear Candidate,

Thank you for your enquiry. Please find enclosed an application pack for the
Director General, Workforce post. Apologies for the delay in letting you have
this information, however we have extended the closing date to Friday 5 May
to account for this. I look forward to hearing from you.

Kind regards,

Robert Jones
02079725861

Mark Hebblewhite
Belmont Hill
Douglas
Isle of Man

Strictly Private and Confidential
Robert Jones
The Department of Health
Corporate Human Resources
Room 286d
Skipton House
80 London Road
London
SE1 6LH

25th April 2006

Dear Robert

Thank you for the application pack which I have put back in the post for you today. Thank you also for extending the closing date – I did not realise I had missed it as I have been busy in the garden. There is a bare patch of grass where the cats go to the toilet and it needed a thorough reseeding. Anyway, to business, I have not included a copy of my CV as it is far too detailed. However, I am willing to concede that I am a fully trained Town Crier who has been operating my own Leisure Balloon Flight Company for the past 10 days. OOOOOOOOOOOOOHHHHHHHHHHHHHHH YYYYYEEEEEEEEYYYYY!!!!!!!!!!!!!!!!!!!

I have had a good read through of the enclosed Civil Service Code that you kindly sent to me via the postman and I can see no problem with me adhering to any of the attached conditions of service and in fact I can be very confidential when the need arises. If someone told me something confidential I would not say nuffink as they would never tell you anything again and a lack of trust in a working relationship, as you know, can lead to enforced reactionary behaviourist principles being supplanted as a consequence of irrational cognitive thought processes resulting in unnecessary and inappropriate signal-response mechanisms coming into play, as occurred when my dad refused to let me watch 'The Land That

Time Forgat' (or 'Forgot', I forget/forgat which). Anyway, I hope my application is successful and I look forward to working with you in the near future. Perhaps we could go out for a few drinks after work. By the way, is there a drinks machine/assorted chilled snacks available in the staffroom?

Yours sincerely

Mark Hebblewhite.

Mark Hebblewhite

Name MARK JOHN HEBBLEWHITE

Survey of Disabilities

Do you consider yourself to have a disability?   Yes ☐   No ☑
   (view the guidance notes below for definition of disability)

Are you applying under the Guaranteed Interview Scheme?   Yes ☑ .... No ☐
(see candidate leaflet for information about this scheme)

To help us classify our results, please tick the box or boxes which best describe your disability.
(view guidance notes below on the associated disability)

Visual impairment   ☐

Hearing impairment   ☐

Speech impairment   ☐

Walking impairment   ☑   WHEN I BLINK I

Physical co-ordination impairment   ☐✗   AM UNABLE TO CONTROL MY LEFT ARM, I NO LONGER VISIT CAFES.

Reduced physical capacity   ☐

Severe disfigurement   ☑

Learning difficulties   ☐

Mental Illness   ☑

Progressive Conditions   ☐

Neurological Conditions   ☐

Other   ☑
please describe

TOE FRACTURED WHILST LOOKING AT MODEL OF 'CROMPTON'S MULE' ON RECENT VISIT TO STAFFORDSHIRE. GETTING BETTER THOUGH ALTHOUGH I AM FINDING IT DIFFICULT TO GET TO THE CHIP SHOP

Name ....Mark Hebblewhite....

NATIONALITY

The information you give us about your nationality is treated as confidential and will be kept separate from your application. This information will be used by Human Resources staff only to confirm your eligibility for applying for Civil Service appointments. Once the recruitment exercise has been completed, this information will be analysed used by Human Resources staff to confirm the standard pre-appointment enquiries for the successful applicant(s).

Nationality at Birth ..British........ **Present Nationality** ....?.........................

Have you ever possessed any other nationality or citizenship?	YES ☐ NO ☑
If yes, give full details with dates	
Are you subject to UK immigration control?	YES ☐ NO ☑
If yes, do you have an unrestricted entitlement to take up employment in the UK?	YES ☐ NO ☑

NOT AT WEEKENDS AS I PLAY DARTS

NON EC NATIONALS ONLY

DETAILS OF WIFE OR HUSBAND (CURRENT PARTNERS ONLY). DO **NOT** COMPLETE IF HE/SHE IS DECEASED OR IF YOU ARE DIVORCED.

NATIONALITY AT BIRTH   VARIABLE   DATE OF MARRIAGE   LIVING WITH PARTNER

CURRENT NATIONALITY   EMPLOYMENT LOCATION   DEPENDENT UPON
                                          LOCATION OF BURGER
                                          VAN

Name: MARK HEBBLEWHITE   Date of Birth ... 04 / 11 / 72

Survey of Ethnic Background

Please look at all the descriptions of race or ethnic background listed below. When you
have read them all, please tick ONE box *in column A AND column B* that most accurately
describes your race or ethnic origin.

Column A - Nationality

Which Group do you most identify with? Choose
from the list below.

(A)	☐	British or Mixed British
(B)	☐	English
(C)	✓	Irish
(D)	☐	Scottish
(E)	☐	Welsh
(F)	☐	Or any other? (specify if you wish)

FAMILY SECRET, CAN'T SAY

Column B - Ethnicity

What is your ethnic Group? Choose
from the list below.

ASIAN

(A)	☐	Bangladeshi
(B)	☐	Indian
(C)	☐	Pakistani
(D)	☐	Any other Asian background (specify if you wish)

....

BLACK

(E)	☐	African
(F)	✓	Caribbean
(G)	☐	Any other Black background (specify if you wish)

....

CHINESE

(H)	✓	Any Chinese background (specify if you wish)

....

MIXED ETHNIC BACKGROUND

(I)	✓	Asian and White
(J)	☐	Black African and White
(K)	☐	Black Caribbean and White
(L)	☐	Any other Mixed ethnic background (specify if you wish)

....

WHITE

(M)	✓	Any White background (specify if you wish)

....

ANY OTHER ETHNIC BACKGROUND

(N)	☐	Any other ethnic background (specify if you wish)

BROUGHT UP BY WOLVES

 **Department of Health**

Skipton House
80 London Road
LONDON
SE1 6LH

Tel: 020 7972 2000
Direct Line: 020 7972
5861

RESTRICTED - PERSONAL
Mark Hebblewhite

Douglas
Isle of Man

10 May 2006

Dear *Mark*

DIRECTOR GENERAL - WORKFORCE

I am writing to acknowledge your application for the post of Director General - Workforce.

A shortlist meeting will take place on 15th May and interviews will be held on Monday 12th June.

Shortlisted candidates will be asked to meet with Professor Clive Fletcher, prior to the formal interview panel, for psychometric assessment. Clive will meet you individually and the assessment is likely to take up to 4 hours. I will work with you to find a convenient date in your diary without, I hope, causing you too much inconvenience.

The selection panel will consist of Bronwen Curtis, Civil Service Commissioner, Hugh Taylor, Acting Permanent Secretary, Sir Ian Carruthers, Acting Chief Executive, and Dame Gill Morgan, Chief Executive of the NHS Confederation. Bronwen will chair the selection panel.

I would be very grateful if you could note the interview date in your diary.

Thank you again for your application and please let me know if you need any further information at this stage.

Yours sincerely

ROBERT JONES
SENIOR CIVIL SERVICE UNIT – CORPORATE HUMAN RESOURCES

Department of Health

Skipton House
80 London Road
London
SE1 6LH

Tel: 020 7972 2000
Direct Line: 020 7972 **5823**

16 May 2006

Dear Mark

DIRECTOR GENERAL - WORKFORCE
DEPARTMENT OF HEALTH

Thank you for your application for the post of Director General - Workforce. I am sorry to have to tell you that you were not shortlisted on this occasion.

It might help to know that the shortlist panel considered your experience and skills in relation to the requirements of the post as set out in the advertisement and candidate leaflet. The panel considered, based on the paper evidence provided, that you did not meet the minimum advertised criteria to warrant an interview under the guaranteed interview scheme on this occasion.

I am sorry to be sending disappointing news.

Yours sincerely

Frances Gillick

FRANCES J GILLICK
Senior Civil Service unit – Corporate Human Resources

Mark Hebblewhite
Belmont Hill
Douglas
Isle of Man

The British Goose Producers Association
Europoint House
5 Lavington Street
London
SE1 ONZ

16th April 2006

Dear Sir or Madam

I have been passed your address by my careers officer who said I should writ to you to ask your advise.

I would verymuch like to learn to be a raise gooses when I leave school but it is very difficult to find infrormation on the subject. I do not want to have an office job as I like to be outdoors. The farmer who lives next door says I can use a small piece of his land for free and then start paying him rent once I start makeing money. Do you mind if I ask you a few questions. How many gooses do I need to start off with and where do I get them from so I know they are proper and healthy, I have been told that you have to check their gums for signs of tooth desease. Also what is the best thing to feed them on and how long is it before I can sell them and how much are they worth and do they need to be kept inside. Thank you very much for your help and I hope to her from you soon.

Yours sincerely

Mark Hebblewhite.

Mark Hebblewhite

British Poultry Council Ltd
Europoint House
5-11 Lavington Street
London SE1 0NZ

Tel: +44 (0)20 7202 4760
Fax: +44 (0)20 7928 6366
e-mail: bpc@poultry.uk.com
website: www.poultry.uk.com

19/04/06

Mr Mark Hebblewhite

Douglas
Isle of Man

Dear Mr. Hebblewhite,

Thank you very much for your interest in the work of the British Goose Sector Group. Please find enclosed an application form for membership, further information on the Group and a list of useful websites and books for new goose producers.

The goose group is a sector within the British Poultry Council; we are a voluntary trade association funded entirely by members' subscriptions. Membership of the British Poultry Council includes companies and individuals engaged in breeding, hatching, rearing and processing chickens, turkeys, ducks and geese to produce poultry meat.

Turning to your letter, it is heartening to hear that there are still people who wish to make a life for themselves in agriculture and the rearing of livestock for quality meat.

To quickly answer your questions, you can start with as many geese as your site allows in terms of stocking density under government welfare regulations; for geese raised in barns with access to light and dry runs this is 15kg/m2 per goose, whilst for a fully free range bird this is 15kg/m2 per goose in its housing and 4kg/m2 in terms of the range for the birds to be out on. I can help talk you through this if necessary.

You should draw up a site plan and understand where the birds will need shedding, water and feeding. You may also need to work out a business case that allows you to understand how many geese are necessary for you to be working on a commercial scale and turning a profit.

There are a very finite number of goose hatcheries in the UK and the majority are members of our group – I list them below and you can have every confidence in them:

Mr Eddie Hegarty – Norfolk Geese – 01379 676391

Dr Anne Ashington - B & A Ashington – 01603 714152

The voice of the British poultry meat sector
Registered in England and Wales no. 916059

Member of a.v.e.c. ◇ Association of European Poultry Industry

British Poultry Council Ltd
Europoint House
5-11 Lavington Street
London SE1 0NZ

Tel: +44 (0)20 7202 4760
Fax: +44 (0)20 7928 6366
e-mail: bpc@poultry.uk.com
website: www.poultry.uk.com

In answering your final questions I have included in this pack a draft copy of the goose producer's code of practice and an outline of traditional goose rearing.

Mr Hegarty and Dr Ashington will be able to amplify the information these documents provide. The British Goose Sector Group has over 50 members and **IS** goose production in the UK – it is a useful and co-operative group who keep in close touch and think of themselves very much as a family, whether a member is producing 50 birds or 5000!

I wish you every success in rearing geese and should you wish to join our group you would be most welcome,

Yours sincerely,

Jeremy Blackburn
Executive Officer

Secretary – British Goose Sector Group

Mark Hebblewhite
Belmont Hill
Douglas
Isle of Man

Jeremy Blackburn
British Goose Sector Group
British Poultry Council
Europoint House
5 Lavington Street
London
SE1 ONZ

24th April 2006

Dear Mrs Blackburn

Thank you for your letter that I got on Saturday regarding my rearing of the gooses. And thank you for all the information you sent me as well. I have bourt 30 gooses since I received your letter and I do keep them in a large barn at the mement that I am renting from the farmer next door their water is in an old bath and I understand from the farmer that they can only eat sausages when after they are six weeks. Yes. I paid 2 puonds 20 for each gooseling

I intend to keep them fully free range and their run will be ready by Thursday as I am going to use an old one that the farmer had when he had gooses but now he just does carrots and potatoes ect. It needs some repareing but it is old but it is good and the wire is broke a bit but its ok because it is nearly all mended. I did show your letter to my careers officer and he said that it was very good of you to replie so propteley. I would very much like to join your association but I will wait until the first ones are reared so I can offord the membership properly if that is ok. My careers officer will be helping me for the first 6 months while I get going and he said he was going to right to someone to thank you about how helpful you have been.

Thank you once more and I hope to hear from you soon. Thank you for youre encouragement and sorry to trouble you but can I send you some diaggrems of the gooses run to check it is ok, my careers officer said that it wss polite to ask first but the farmer said just send them but I thought I would ask as the careers officer said not to lisen to the farmer as he is a joker.

Yours sincerely

Mark Hebblewhite.

Mark Hebblewhite

BRITISH GOOSE SECTOR GROUP
EUROPOINT HOUSE, 5 LAVINGTON STREET LONDON, SE1 0NZ
Tel: +44 (0)207 202 4760 Fax: +44 (0) 207 928 6366
E-Mail: bpc@poultry.uk.com Website: www.goose.cc

Mr Mark Hebblewhite

Douglas
Isle of Man

03 May 2006

Dear Mr Hebblewhite,

Thank you for your letter of the 25th April. My apologies for not replying quicker but as you may well have guessed my office has been rather busy with both the H5N1 avian flu positive swan in Scotland and the more recent outbreak of H7N3 on several farms in Norfolk.

Your letter sounds encouraging and I'm glad you're making progress. You make a good point in waiting until you've had a successful crop of geese before thinking about spending the money to join our Goose Group. I would emphasise that point in fact, that your rearing of geese must turn a profit in order for you to make a successful farming business.

It's good to see you are thinking about the health and welfare of your geese as well, that's a key responsibility of every stockman. This is essential for giving them a good life until slaughtered but also because a well reared bird will make for good meat and a higher selling price.

If you work to the draft code I sent you and follow the traditional British method of rearing free range geese, as well as doing your own site planning, I am sure that you will become a successful goose farmer.

I would be happy to look over any map or plan and would forward a copy to either the Chairman or Vice-Chairman of our group for their opinion too. Perhaps you might also get your Careers Officer to give me a call?

I look forward to hearing from you and wish you every success with your goose business,

Jeremy Blackburn

Jeremy Blackburn
Secretary – British Goose Sector Group

Mr Victor Williams
Belmont Hill
Douglas
Isle of Man

Jeremy Blackburn
British Goose Sector Group
British Poultry Council
Europoint House
5 Lavington Street
London
SE1 0NZ

25ᵗʰ April 2006

Dear Mr Blackburn

I am writing to thank you for your assistance with a project one of my former students is undertaking regarding the rearing of geese. As I am sure you have guessed, Mark is very easily led – however, he has been greatly enthused by his correspondence with yourself relating to his chosen career.

Despite his tendency to be easily misled he has displayed a remarkable talent with animals and his commitment to this project is second to none. Indeed since your initial letter he has been working around the clock in order to ensure the currently run-down accommodation for the animals is brought up to scratch. Mark's aptitude for his new job has surprised all of his former teachers. However, I have stressed to him that his business is a commercial venture and to that end it would be best if he did not get too attached to the animals in question and that it would be best if he did not give them names, bearing in mind their eventual fate. If you do have any further correspondence with Mark please would it be possible for you to reinforce this point as I think he would heed advice from yourself as a professional in the industry.

Thank you once again for the time and effort you have taken in assisting Mark in his venture. It is greatly appreciated and all of Mark's former teachers including myself think that the time and effort you are giving him in order that he succeed in his chosen career is commendable.

Yours faithfully

Victor Williams

Victor Williams

BRITISH GOOSE SECTOR GROUP
EUROPOINT HOUSE, 5 LAVINGTON STREET LONDON, SE1 0NZ
Tel: +44 (0)207 202 4760 Fax: +44 (0) 207 928 6366
E-Mail: bpc@poultry.uk.com Website: www.goose.cc

Mr Victor Williams
Ground Floor Flat
4 Sartfell Road
Douglas
Isle of Man

03 May 2006

Dear Mr Williams,

Thank you for your letter of the 25th April. My apologies for not replying quicker but as you may well have guessed my office has been rather busy with both the H5N1 positive swan in Scotland and the more recent outbreak of H7N3 on several farms in Norfolk.

Your letter clarified Mark's situation, though I had pretty much gathered this from his correspondence. I will of course reply to him and help in whatever way I can. He is also lucky that my group of goose producers really do see themselves as a 'family' and try to encourage new members. It's a sad fact that I couldn't offer the same for chicken, turkey and duck sector groups but these are multi-million pound agri-businesses and not smallholders.

I will re-emphasise to Mark the commercial nature of his rearing of geese; he seems to be getting similar advice too from a farmer. It's key that he meets all the animal health and welfare requirements of his birds, not only to comply with industry best practice, but for when he gets inspected by an Environmental Health Officer. A healthy, well reared bird is also a good selling bird.

Mark refers to what his careers officer thinks of this farmer in his letter to me and I must admit that I wouldn't want any new goose producer to fall into old fashioned ways of farming or treating animals. By what you've said I think Mark could easily become both a model stockman and successful smallholder; I hope that you and Mark's careers officer can make sure he gets the right sources of advice on the Isle of Man.

I wish Mark every success and look forward to his joining our British Goose Sector Group; please keep me informed of how he is getting on and how things progress,

Jeremy Blackburn

Jeremy Blackburn
Secretary – British Goose Sector Group

Mr Victor Williams
Belmont Hill
Douglas
Isle of Man

Jeremy Blackburn
British Goose Sector Group
British Poultry Council
Europoint House
5 Lavington Street
London
SE1 0NZ

6th May 2006

Dear Mr Blackburn

Thank you for your letter of 3rd May regarding Mark. I am extremely pleased that you are continuing to support Mark in his enterprise with your advice as to correct practice and current legislation. I would like to take this opportunity to reassure you that both I and Mr Hope, (Mark's careers officer) are doing the utmost to ensure that Mark's activities are correctly supervised, although at present I am doing the majority of the supervision as Mr Hope is recovering from a tracheotomy. The farmer Mark may have mentioned in his letters, Mr Smythe is a well-intentioned soul but prone to teasing with Mark that can sometimes get out of hand. Be assured that Mark's geese are in the very best of hands at all times. Thank you once again for your assistance.

Yours faithfully

Victor Williams

Victor Williams

Mark Hebblewhite
Belmont Hill
Douglas
Isle of Man

Roger Williams
United Kingdom Warehousing Association
Walter House
418-422 Strand
London
WC2R 0PT

16th April 2006

Dear Mr Williams

I am writing to invite you to an event on 27th July. To get straight to the point, I am president of The Carry On Films Appreciation Society (formed 1973) and one of the group's members, Joyce Stanton, has been undertaking some research as regards the family trees of some of the leading cast members. When Joyce discovered that you were related to Kenneth Williams we thought it appropriate to invite you to attend our AGM and perhaps if you could be persuaded, to give a short talk and recollection of your memories of the great man himself. I am sure that this is not the first time you have been asked to attend such an event to speak about your famous relative. However, it would mean a great deal to the society if you were able to attend. We would of course pay for your flights and accommodation for three days for yourself and a companion – however, we are only able to pay a modest fee (by negotiation). I look forward to hearing from you if you are able to accept our invitation, and in the words of the great man himself, oooh matron!

Yours sincerely

Mark Hebblewhite.

Mark Hebblewhite

UKWA united kingdom
warehousing association

Walter House   418-422 Strand   London   WC2R OPT   T (020) 7836 5522   F (020) 7438 9379

E-mail dg@ukwa.org.uk   Web www.ukwa.org.uk

Mark Hepplewhite

Douglas
Isle of Man

21 April 2006

Dear Mark,

Thank you for your letter dated 16 April 2006 in which you invite me to attend the AGM of the Carry on Films Appreciation Society on 27 July 2006. It would, I am sure, be a pleasure to attend your meeting, but your invitation has me a little bewildered, and tempted me to say…. *'Stop messing about!'* . I am no expert on family trees, and I have done no deliberate research into my own family history. However, as far as I am aware Kenneth Williams is not related to me, and I am intrigued to know how Joyce Stanton has reached that conclusion.

She may be right, but if so, I have been in blissful ignorance of the relationship, and never had the pleasure of meeting Kenneth. I fear therefore that I am ill equipped to talk with any authority about him, unless I start my research now!!

I suspect Joyce has uncovered the 'wrong' Roger Williams, but if she wants to quiz me further, please get her to call me. My office number is 02078365522. Good luck in your search.

Kind regards

Roger Williams

MEMBER OF THE
EUROPEAN WAREHOUSING
AND LOGISTICS CONFEDERATION

President: Lord Brabazon of Tara
Director General: R.J.Willems

MEMBER OF THE
INTERNATIONAL FEDERATION OF
WAREHOUSING LOGISTICS ASSOCIATIONS

Mark Hebblewhite
Belmont Hill
Douglas
Isle of Man

Roger Williams
United Kingdom Warehousing Association
Walter House
418-422 Strand
London
WC2R 0PT

24th April 2006

Dear Roger

Thank you for your letter dated 21st April 2006. I have asked Joyce Stanton to recheck her findings and without wanting to shock you it would appear that you are indeed a relative of Kenneth. At the time of my initial invitation we were not aware that you had not met the man himself. However, our invitation still stands if you are interested. If it is of any use I can put you in touch with Debbie Hawtry, 2nd cousin of Charles, or Lee Breslaw, Bernard's brother, both of whom are also attending the AGM for the third time and who may be able to assist you with your presentation should you desire to proceed with the invite. Relatives of the gifted ones are always welcomed at our events and indeed are held in some esteem. We would of course understand if you did not desire to further your involvement and in that case please accept my apologies on behalf of the organisation for my intrusion. I would be happy to forward a copy of your family tree for your perusal should you wish to appear at our event but I regret Joyce is unable to contact you by telephone with further details as she is a mute. I am sorry if my initial letter has shocked you in any way but in no way was this the intention as so far as my organisation was concerned your link to the great man although not publicised, has always been in the public domain and may be viewed at your local public records office. Once again I hope you are able to attend our event and I hope to hear from you once you have been able to clarify Joyce's findings. Please feel free to contact me if you require any further details and/or a copy of the said family tree.

Best wishes

Mark Hebblewhite.

Mark Hebblewhite

Mark Hebblewhite
Belmont Hill
Douglas
Isle of Man

Weight Watchers UK Ltd
Customer Services Department
Millennium House
Ludlow Road
Maidenhead
Berkshire
SL6 2SL

22nd April 2006

Dear Sir or Madam

My new year's resolution was to lose at least 3 stone before I go on holiday in August this year. We are going to Tenerife and I can't wait to get to the beach and not be embarrassed. I am currently 18 stone and 4ft 9 tall and I would like to get to a trim and healthy 15 stone. I have given up crisps and chocolate and since New Year's Eve. I have lost 2 stone which I think is fantastic, a great start I think you will agree. It would be great if your organisation could support me in my healthy eating and exercise programme. Do you have any literature to assist me in planning healthy menus? Or any keep fit regimes? I am currently walking 2 miles per day, the first time I have walked anywhere for a while. I have to turn left when I reach the end of my road as there are three shops if I turn right and this way I am able to avoid them. I look forward to hearing from you and I do hope you are able to support me during this difficult period.

Best wishes

Mark Hebblewhite.

Mark Hebblewhite

ℂWeightWatchers®

Weight Watchers (UK) Ltd. Customer Service Department, Millennium House,
Ludlow Road, Maidenhead, Berkshire, SL6 2SL
Telephone 0845 345 1500

Mr. Mark Hebblewhite

Douglas
ISLE OF MAN
Isle Of Man

28 April 2006

Dear Mark

Well done on a fantastic weight loss so far.

By joining Weight Watchers you will be given expert advice on healthy eating,
suggested menu plans and exercise whilst following our revolutionary new weight
loss programme, Switch. With new Switch you'll discover how to make the right
small changes, one step at a time. Changes you can actually make because they're
based on your lifestyle. The only big change will be to your weight. And, for the
first time ever, there's a choice of two food plans - and you can even switch
between them. So you lose weight eating the way you want to eat.
With the brand new NoCount™ plan, you eat freely and healthily from a
comprehensive list of foods. You even get a weekly POINTS® allowance for snacks
and treats.
Full Choice is based on the proved POINTS system, but with a difference; you now
have a new personalised daily POINTS allowance.
Switch is not magic. But by giving you as much choice as possible so that you can
base the programme around you and your life, you now have a better chance of
success than ever before.

If you would like details of your nearest Meeting then please call our Meeting
Information Line on 08457 123000 or visit our web site at
www.weightwatchers.co.uk and click on 'find a meeting'.

We wish you great success with the programme.

Yours sincerely
WEIGHT WATCHERS UK LTD

Registered Office: Weight Watchers (UK) Ltd. Millennium House, Ludlow Road, Maidenhead, Berkshire SL6 2SL.
Registered in England and Wales No. 1248588 VAT No. 578 3845 85 • Tel: 01628 777 077   Fax: 01628 415 263

Kevin Cubbage
Builders Merchants Federation
15 Soho Square
London
W1D 3HL

16th April 2006

Dear Kevin

I am writing to ask for your assistance as a leading authority on construction materials.

On 14th June I am hosting a small party to celebrate my wife's birthday. She works in Bakers Oven and so to surprise her I am constructing (or rather attempting to) a giant sausage roll as a centrepiece for the living room. I have tried all sorts of materials, including a length of tree trunk wrapped up in a cream rug, but it does not look right. Please can you advise me of the best (and cheapest) way of constructing this sausage roll since you have the knowledge to make my idea become reality? Please get back to me ASAP.

Yours sincerely

Mark Hebblewhite.

Mark Hebblewhite

Builders Merchants Federation

Mark Hebblewhite

Douglas
Isle of Man

21 April 2006

Dear Mr Hebblewhite,

Thank you for your letter of the 16th of April addressed to our Chairman Kevin Cubbage.

I regret that in this instance we cannot be of any help to you.

Yours sincerely,

Jeremy Hawksley
Managing Director

15 Soho Square
London W1D 3HL
Tel: 0870 901 3380
Fax: 020 7734 2766
Email: info@bmf.org.uk
www.bmf.org.uk

**Building a better
Supply Chain**

INVESTOR IN PEOPLE

Mark Hebblewhite
Belmont Hill
Douglas
Isle of Man

The Geologists' Association
Burlington House
Piccadilly
London
W1J 0BJ

17th April 2006

Dear Sir or Madam

I wonder if you would be able to help me with a query. I have been passed your address by a work colleague who has attended university and he said you could possibly assist me. I am trying to establish the approximate age of an animal skeleton I have uncovered in my back garden whilst I was laying a new patio. I have heard that it is possible to date items by looking at rock layers surrounding them and this being the case would you be able to assist me?

The remains were uncovered at a depth of 1 and a half feet and it appears that there are 2 layers of material above them. One is a brownish coloured moist layer, followed by a hard yellow/brown layer approximately 1 ft in depth. The remains themselves are in this hard yellow/brown layer and underneath that there appears to be a layer of hard white rock. How old would you estimate the remains to be and is there any way of verifying this? My work colleague has informed me that I could have made an important discovery and has urged me to contact a local museum. However, I would rather seek a second opinion first. Also what animal do you think the skeleton could come from? Since it is buried so deep (1 and a half feet) it has been suggested that it could date back to the middle ages or before.

The skeleton itself is in one piece, there are four or five legs and the skull appears to be the same size as a small orange although it is not the same colour. There is a small bell and a piece of fabric buried besides the skeleton and my work colleague has informed me that it is possible that this means the burial had some form of religious significance and could date back to something he called the reformation which I believe had something to do with King Henry the Eighth. I have covered my find with a blue tarpaulin weighed down with rocks so it can be preserved until you get back to me with some advice. Thank you very much in anticipation of your assistance.

Yours sincerely

Mark Hebblewhite.

Mark Hebblewhite

GEOLOGY

25/04/06

Dear Mark,

Sarah of the GA Office has passed on your query about the skeleton to me, and I will try to tease out options. It is fortunate that the bones are still articulated – very often they are scattered in a way which adds to the problem of identification.

I don't think the soil/sediment layers will help too much in this case unless they were extended over a wider area than your garden or had artefacts such as coins or pottery which would say "medieval" or "Roman". So we are left with identification.

I once had a book 'Bones for Archaeologists' which was excellent for small mammals or distinguishing aurochs from ordinary cow, sheep as opposed to goat. As would be the case, I can't find it at present!

Four or five legs puzzles me. Could it be a long tail? What about paws? Claws? When you say "skull same size as small orange", could it be Cat? Teeth would be important. Sharp incisors + evidence of a carnivore

Could the bell & fabric be the remains of a collar? Sorry if all of this sounds a put-down and too obvious.

You have done all we would ask of anyone making a find, and seeking a museum comment. We 'doctors' need to see the patient to be positive, so all of this is conjecture on my part!

For the Isle of Man, you have the Manx Heritage Museum

Editor
Peter Doyle
Geology Today
Geological Society of London
Burlington House
Piccadilly
London W1J 0BG, UK

Email: doyle268@btinternet.com

Assistant Editor
Eric Robinson
Riverside Farm
Whitehall
Watchet TA23 0BB, UK
Tel: 01984 639390

Published by Blackwell Publishing Ltd
in association with the Geological
Society and the Geologists'
Association

in Douglas where the Keeper used to be Dr C S. Garrard who also covered Geology, but, we also have a GA member in Lady Eva Wilson in the ~~████████████~~, who had Natural History Museum experience when she lived in London. She would be a contact if you wanted a second opinion on your find. She retired to Man when her husband David Wilson stood down as Director of the British Museum in Bloomsbury some years back. A viking specialist, he also is a palaeontologist.

   Good luck with your enquiries

Eric Robinson

Vice Pres. Royal Archaeological Institute

Mark Hebblewhite
Belmont Hill
Douglas
Isle of Man

Eric Robinson
Vice President
Royal Archaeological Institute
Riverside Farm
Whitehall
Watchet
TA23 0BB

1st May 2006

Dear Eric

Thank you for your letter dated 25th April with regard to the unidentified remains discovered in my garden during recent construction work (patio) carried out by myself. Please would you pass my thanks on to Sarah at the Geologists' Association for being so kind as to forward my letter.

Good news is two-fold in that I think I have been able to identify the said remains and also the patio is complete. Indeed I have just finished coating the table and chairs in linseed oil and they have been set up on their new firm foundation above the resting place of the discovery. I have taken heed of the your comments regarding the possible existence of a tail (as opposed to a fifth leg) and also the clue you gave me regarding claws and I have come to the following conclusions.

The musculoskeletal system of the animal bears many similarities to that of the species Felis silvestris (cat). Furthermore I believe I may be able to give you some insight into the cause of death. There is a small fracture in the scapular 4cm above the humerus and also evidence of partial severance in the cranial border of the tibia, although curiously enough the fibula is unaffected. I would suggest, therefore, that it is possible that a fall occurred prior to the burial, possibly from the apple tree that borders the fence which is a common roosting spot for a variety of birds. In terms of a date of demise I would suggest that the animal expired in approximately 2004 since I have been reliably informed that the small bell and fabric are the remains of a collar last manufactured in 2004 by Whiskas, available only on the submission of ten tokens. I do have one remaining query you may be able to assist me with, the answer to which may throw doubt upon the hypotheses I have outlined above. In my previous letter I described the skull as the same size as a small orange. Closer inspection of the 'skull' has led me to the conclusion that it is indeed a small orange and not a skull at all. Are you aware of any carnivorous mammals that do not have heads and display a fondness for citrus fruits? Thank you for your interest in my excavation and if I can assist you in identifying any remains in your garden please do not hesitate to contact me. I look forward to your comments on my investigation and I would be pleased to hear from you soon.

Yours sincerely

Mark Hebblewhite.

Mark Hebblewhite

Mark Hebblewhite
Belmont Hill
Douglas
Isle of Man

Washerhelp
Washing Machine Repairs
46 Oxted Road
Sheffield
South Yorkshire
S9 1BP

24th April 2006

Dear Sir

I have been passed your address by the manager of Currys in Rotherham (where my wife and I have our holiday home) who said you might be able to assist me. I have been repairing washing machines on a continuous basis since 1984 and it would also be fair to say the job has become a bit of a hobby as well. In June myself and a colleague, Peter, are attending a trade event in Nottingham (all the big names will be there) to deliver a humorous role play and mime based on the moment the Beatty brothers in Ontario realised that washing machines based on an agitating process were the way forward. The performance ends with a laugh when Peter drops a pretend ribbed copper and chromium plated tub on his toe whilst effecting a repair! Could I ask if you would consider assisting to promote the event by providing us with a quotation regarding the performance that would be used on the flyer that is to be handed out at the event? If possible I would like to send you a copy of the script for your comments.

Myself and Peter would be very grateful for your assistance and I hope to hear from you soon.

Kind regards

Mark Hebblewhite.

Mark Hebblewhite

Washerhelp.co.uk
46 Oxted Road
Brightside
Sheffield
S9 1BP
South Yorkshire
Tel: 0114 2433111 Email: andy@washerhelp.com

All things (UK) washing machine related

May 9, 2006

Dear Mark

Sorry I haven't replied before. I'm not used to the old technology of writing letters and kept putting it aside until later. I hope you have access to a computer because it's so much easier to send emails. I don't know what the event is, and can't comment on the performance as I don't know anything about it either. Can you send me more details?

Andy Trigg
Web Master & Publisher

Mark Hebblewhite
Belmont Hill
Douglas
Isle of Man

The School Library Association
Lotmead Business Village
Lotmead Farm
Wanborough
Swindon
SN4 0UY

25th April 2006

Dear Sir or Madam

I have been employed as a school librarian for 12 years now and although I am not a member of your organisation I would like to submit an idea to you. To celebrate my retirement on 15th June my wife has paid for me to get a tattoo and I would very much like to get one bearing the name of your organisation to remind me of all the good times I have had over the last 12 years. The design I have in mind has a basic Celtic knot type construction with three intertwined panels which feature the name of your organisation. Would it be possible to send you a copy of my design for your approval before I get it done? Should you like it I would be happy to hand over the design's copyright to yourselves.

Yours sincerely

Mark Hebblewhite.

Mark Hebblewhite

School Library Association

Mr M Hebblewhite

Douglas
Isle of Man

3 May, 2006

Dear Mark,

Thank you for your letter regarding your possible tattoo and permission to use the SLA name as part of this.

I'm sorry that I have to tell you that I don't think this would be possible as we do not permit any use of our name or logo except for organisations we might work with and events we might support. Where our name is used it is always in conjunction with our logo. We also do not permit any amendment to our logo (see above) when used by other people. And of course, if we did grant permission to use our logo, and that should be changed in the future, you would need to change your tattoo which could prove both painful and costly!

Finally I have to say that if you are not and have never been a member I wonder if this would indeed be the most appropriate thing for you to have as part of a tattoo anyway – why not the name of the school where you worked, or even your wife?

Even though this is not going to prove possible I do send you my very best wishes for your retirement.

Yours sincerely

Kathy Lemaire

Kathy Lemaire
Chief Executive

The School Library Association Unit 2 Lotmead Business Village Lotmead Farm
Wanborough Nr. Swindon Wiltshire SN4 0UY

Tel 01793 791787 Fax 01793 791786 e-mail info@SLA.org.uk web www.SLA.org.uk

Chief Executive Kathy Lemaire BA DipLib MCLIP FRSA Registered Charity No. 313660
Incorporated under the Companies Act 1948 as a Company Limited by Guarantee Registered in England No. 552476 at Lotmead Business Village Wiltshire SN4 0UY

With thanks to all the great sports who made this book possible by allowing me to include their correspondence. I would also like to thank my inquisitive postman, who has been amazed at the volume of letters I have received; Pirjo, whom I ignored for 12 months while I was busy writing to people I had never heard of; and everyone at Summersdale for their help with this book.

www.summersdale.com